PENGUIN BUSINESS
THE ART OF MANAGEMENT

Shiv Shivakumar, or Shiv, as he is popularly known, is one of India's longest-serving CEOs. He is currently the group executive president at Aditya Birla Group. He has worked across multiple industries and categories, and has handled over sixty brands in his career. He was the CEO for Nokia in India and subsequently led the company's emerging markets unit. He was also the chairman and CEO for PepsiCo South Asia. He is ranked among India's leading management and leadership thinkers and speakers. He is the author of the bestselling *The Right Choice*, which was published by Penguin Random House India in 2021.

THE
ART
OF MANAGEMENT

MANAGING YOURSELF

MANAGING YOUR TEAM

MANAGING YOUR BUSINESS

SHIV SHIVAKUMAR

FOREWORD BY
SACHIN TENDULKAR

BUSINESS

An imprint of Penguin Random House

PENGUIN BUSINESS

USA | Canada | UK | Ireland | Australia
New Zealand | India | South Africa | China

Penguin Business is part of the Penguin Random House group of companies
whose addresses can be found at global.penguinrandomhouse.com

Published by Penguin Random House India Pvt. Ltd
4th Floor, Capital Tower 1, MG Road,
Gurugram 122 002, Haryana, India

Penguin
Random House
India

First published in Penguin Business by Penguin Random House India 2022

ISBN 9780670096893

Typeset in Adobe Garamond Pro by Manipal Technologies Limited, Manipal
Printed at Replika Press Pvt. Ltd, India

www.penguin.co.in

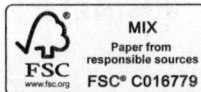

MIX
Paper from
responsible sources
FSC
www.fsc.org   FSC® C016779

This is my third book, and it is dedicated to:

All those who taught and inspired me and raised the bar—my teachers, my mentors and my colleagues.

'Thank you' is really a small phrase to repay a huge debt!

Contents

Foreword

I have known Shiv for many years now. We have met at the sidelines of sporting events and brand launches. He has led diverse businesses and teams, and brings in a wealth of experience. When Shiv told me that he was writing a book about team management and self-management, I thought it was apt. Youngsters can learn from his knowledge and experience accumulated over the years.

As a prelude to the book, Shiv asked me to pen down my thoughts on various aspects. Having played a team sport all my life, I reflected on the following subjects. Shiv, I am sure, has covered these topics in detail through the book.

Discipline and Managing One's Emotions

To manage oneself in all aspects of life, one needs discipline. I attribute my early discipline to my brother, Ajit. He taught me that discipline comes from paying attention to smaller things, like packing my cricket kit carefully and ensuring that my clothes and cricket gear were clean.

Discipline knows no boundaries, whether it's the professional sphere or the personal sphere. It's either there or it isn't. As an analogy, think of a tree: the visible, beautiful parts of a tree are its branches, leaves and flowers, and one is tempted to water them. But its roots are the key; without the roots there is no branch or flower. If you want your tree to grow and blossom, you need to take care of the roots.

Managing Expectations

Expectations are a result of one's actions and track record. When one has done good things or achieved something in the past, it is natural for people to expect more from one. In fact, I would feel bad if people did not expect anything but the best from me. As a professional in any sphere, it would be odd to experience indifference to you or your work. Expectations motivated me; they gave rise to pressure, but pressure need not be construed as negative—it can spur you to do better.

If I ever imagined the weight of a billion people on my shoulders, I would have probably collapsed. But that was not how I saw it. I saw the collective force of a billion people behind me, pushing me forward. What can be more motivating and helpful than a billion-plus Indians propelling me towards my team's goals and my goals?

Handling Criticism

Criticism is a part and parcel of life. One must be open to constructive criticism. We tend to label people, and hence we notice the label first and then the suggestion. I never put a label on anyone—'ex-cricketers', 'journalists', 'commentators' or even my 'fans'. I just saw them as people who were giving me feedback. Believe it or not, it was a waiter at a Chennai hotel who told me that my armguard was coming in the way of my free bat swing! I accepted his feedback, reflected on it and took some corrective steps, and it helped me.

At the same time, one must know how to move on from discussions about the past. My motto was, 'It's the next ball that matters.' Imagine you are a batter and there are two balls coming at you at 140-plus kmph. One is from the past, something that disturbed you, and the second one is from the real world. If I have to score runs, I have to live in the real world and face the real ball. Therefore, I had to train my mind to forget the past.

Adapting to the Times

Change is a constant in all aspects of life. If I look at cricket, it has changed massively over the years, and to thrive one has had to adapt. The key to adaptability is acceptability. If your mind can't accept the changes, then it won't let the body adapt to newer environments. Once I accepted the changes, I also made it a point to enjoy them. One must be comfortable being uncomfortable. Whether it was a new format, newer conditions or a new mystery bowler, I enjoyed being challenged. I saw everything different as an opportunity to learn something new, and I believe learning should never stop.

When talking to young cricketers, I emphasize the importance of getting the basics right. If the foundation is strong, you can add any number of floors to a building. Similarly, one can adapt to newer formats of cricket, provided the basics have been mastered. If you learn to 'bat', you can bat anywhere—Tests, ODIs or T20. However, if you get carried away and learn to 'hit T20 shots' alone, then your success may be short-lived, and you will not be in a position to prepare yourself for any innovative formats.

Sometimes people tend to think of technique as limiting and orthodox. However, true technique liberates you and prepares you to adapt and win.

On My Second Innings

Who I am today is because of the unconditional love this country has provided. I will always continue batting for India. Giving back to society forms a key part of my second innings. There is a lot that can be done for our children—they are our future. The work being done by my foundation shall, hopefully, speak for itself in the years to come.

We are one of the youngest nations, but not the fittest. Transforming India from a sports-loving nation to a sports-playing nation, by partnering with like-minded stakeholders, has been another focus.

Brands are part of modern culture and have a key role in shaping society too. Partnering with purpose-driven brands, which impact society positively, is very satisfying. My team and I are also excited about technology and what it can do to make life better. I work with technology start-ups and am inspired by the innovative solutions that young entrepreneurs are bringing to the table.

Advice for Youngsters

Irrespective of which profession you are in, never get intimidated by seniors. Always make it a point to share your ideas with the rest of the team and never be afraid of being ridiculed. When you speak your mind, people appreciate the value you bring to the team. I was the youngest member when I joined the team, but I always made it a point to share what I was thinking with my teammates, seniors and captains.

Dreams are the biggest sources of energy. My dream to lift the World Cup started in 1983, and we eventually lifted the World Cup for India in 2011. But it all started with a dream. Chase your dreams—they do come true. If you keep living your dream every day of your life, it will eventually turn into reality one day.

January 2022   Sachin Tendulkar
Mumbai

Introduction

I published *The Right Choice* over fifteen months ago. It was an immediate bestseller, and I got some useful feedback from readers. Most agreed with the ten dilemmas I discussed at length in the book and benefitted from the advice given by professionals. However, a lot of readers wrote to me asking about life and work.

I am sure your life went upside down in the pandemic—things you took for granted went missing and things that were unexpected happened. The management of everything in life assumed new and significant digital proportions over the last two years.

Many professionals judge the meaning of their life through the lens of their career and the money they have saved and invested.

But life has changed and so have careers.

Careers and life capabilities required to stay relevant are changing as well. We seem to have endless choices, at least at the start of a career, and we see a faster narrowing of choices after middle management. How does one think about one's own life and career in this changing decade?

Life and careers have changed significantly and will change even more now. There are different analogies, I believe, that one can use three analogies to think of life and careers in this decade. The first is what I label the aircraft flight model; the second is the T20 cricket model; and the third is the shopping mall model.

Let's begin with looking back at the last twenty-four months, which made many of us seek the real meaning of our lives, in the contexts of work, society and progress.

The last two years, 2020 and 2021, posed many challenges to professionals, their lives, their careers and families. The challenges were posed at a larger philosophical level, but also at the level of rethinking the life and career model. Are today's professionals future-ready, considering the way society and the talent markets are changing?

The Great Resignation, in which more than 20 million Americans left their jobs in six months, and the fact that nearly 61 per cent of Indian professionals say that they want to look for a new job in 2022 are not surprising. Professionals are re-evaluating their priorities and their life and career approach. Managing life and career today is different from the past, and that's what I intend to cover in this book. Many of the old principles might still apply, but the way to think about them will be different.

Let's look at some assumptions we have made about life and careers, maybe things we have blindly propagated so far.

Let's start with three questions.

The first is: Is a career in a company valuable? We tended to equate getting into a good company with a visa and saw the company as a place from where one could retire. But 'hire to retire' doesn't exist today. Why so?

The company is no longer a continuing entity in the way we have known it to be. The average life of a company has dropped from about sixty years in the 1960s to about twenty years today, or even less. The average employee tenure in a company is less than four years; the average tenure of CXOs, too, is less than four years.

Things change quickly in a career and sometimes irreversibly. So, staying in a company or in a business unit that might not exist in the future, or gets repositioned, is not a preferred option for professionals.

So the longevity of companies and loyalty of employees are not a happy bundle any more.

Now for the second question: Is the MNC job still attractive and safe?

A lot of people want to join an MNC for its systems, processes, the scope it presents for learning and possible global postings. This might still hold true in a few cases. However, many MNCs have shut shop in emerging markets, and many have sold off their unprofitable or underperforming businesses over time. General Electric (GE) shut down, or got split up. GSK sold Horlicks to Unilever India. Unilever sold Dalda, the edible fats brand, to Bunge and recently tried to get out of the tea business. Electrolux and Philips Consumer Electronics closed down in India. A part of the Citibank consumer business is up for sale.

If you look at the auto sector, General Motors, Ford, Harley Davidson, Fiat, MAN Trucks have all quit India.

PepsiCo franchised its beverages business, and none of the experienced PepsiCo employees stayed in the franchised unit. Pepsico is now transferring the manufacturing of some parts of salty snacks to franchise partners. Pizza Hut and its associated brands were 100 per cent franchised a few years ago, and all the senior and middle managers moved out in new directions.

Carrefour, the French retail giant, has left India, as also the Japanese pharma giant Daiichi Sankyo.

MNCs are deepening their home-base presence and investments this decade. In the 1960s, there were 7000 MNCs globally; in 2006, this number went up to 80,000.* MNCs find it challenging to operate in volatile economic conditions and also in a fluctuating regulatory framework economy. Twenty-five per cent of German-based MNCs are planning to exit China.

GE, one of the world's largest conglomerates, has consistently reshaped its business line and geography focus, so much so that it is now three different companies.

I think this decade, MNCs will look at safe-haven countries and safe-haven categories, and technology MNCs will adapt differently. If technology companies do not adapt to local conditions, we will see the rise of local digital giants.

Now to the third question: Is a series of jobs in start-ups attractive now?

---

* Source: Pankaj Ghemawat and Niccolo Pisani, *Harvard Business Review.*

The start-up space has become attractive but overhyped in the last few years, with technology and direct-to-consumer/ customer business models gaining traction.

Access to technology, access to cloud networks, access to high-quality talent and access to capital have made the start-up ecosystem super competitive vis-à-vis the slow legacy companies.

Legacy companies didn't exploit niches and didn't look to grow niches; they started with a mass idea and stayed with that idea. Start-ups are exploring every niche and making it bigger. A consumption economy helps this immensely.

Any industry that has high physical transaction costs is ripe for digital disruption. We have seen this in books, music, travel, entertainment, etc. The financial sector will see the biggest digital disruption now as in financial services globally, regulation and a benign, helpful central bank were the moats. Now, they will go away, with crypto, the challenge to reserve currencies and decentralized finance.

And finally, the billion-dollar question: How does one manage life and a career in a future world?

The whole discipline of management now has three elements to it:

- Managing Yourself
- Managing Your Team
- Managing Your Business

The big difference from the past, in my view, is that all the three elements are your responsibility today. The company can help, but you are in charge fully, and you need to navigate the turbulent professional arena on your own. So, you need to own this.

I am a sounding board to a number of people—MBA students, young, mid-level and senior managers and entrepreneurs. Everyone I chat with seeks success. The definition of success is invariably a CXO /senior job, and success is associated with fame and money, with money being a proxy for security.

However, not everyone has an idea or a road map to get to their desired success destination. I sense that 'hope' is the biggest life and career management strategy for most people. And hope is never a sustainable strategy.

I ask people to think differently about their life and careers. Let's go back to the analogies I started with: the aircraft flight model, the T20 cricket model and the shopping mall model. Let me explain.

Aircraft Flight Model

Aircraft fly at different altitudes and have a clear, specific destination. Having a sense of your destination, of what you could likely become, is important, as well as having a sense of what drives you and your passion. A pilot navigating an aircraft has a lot of instruments on his dashboard to tell him what's happening and what he should watch out for. Life and careers, too, have similar dashboards, if we care to look for them. There are some important aspects—that direction is more important than the distance covered. Many people want to move up fast, but flying at the right speed at the right time is important.

Aircraft use and manage jet streams to avoid turbulence and ensure a smooth flight. Life and careers are also like that. You need to use the jet stream in a role to get yourself mileage and then move to the next stream that accelerates your progress.

When an aircraft encounters dark clouds and bad weather, the pilot first slows down, reassesses the situation and sees what detours he needs to take to go past the weather hurdle on way to the destination. Life and careers are similar when you face dark clouds. You need to pause and rethink what's happening to you. For this to happen, you need a few emotional anchors, people you can share your situation with, people who will tell you the raw truth while being empathetic. Many people have an ostrich attitude in tough times; they blame their life on karma or the boss or the company.

Life and careers in a future world will have many more dark clouds, and there will be many instances when you will need to fasten your seat belt.

T20 Cricket Model

T20 has revolutionized cricket, and a number of innovations/practices from T20 cricket have now crept into Test cricket as well. Examples include the reverse sweep, slower bouncer, boundary relay catch, high fielding standards, running between the wickets, fitness of the players and, most important of all, the data and the insights from the data.

T20 is a brutal game. Yesterday's captain is tomorrow's twelfth man. Things are never so severe in the corporate world. You need a thick skin when you are a cricketer of the stature of Paul Stirling or Hashim Amla or Joe Root or Steve Smith or Adil Rashid, and you are not picked by any team. Even when picked, you are playing second fiddle. Life can turn out like that when you are on top of it on one day and down in the dumps the next day. Actors go through that in Bollywood and Hollywood.

The captain of a national team could be in the reserves in the Indian Premier League (IPL) team. M.S. Dhoni was dropped from the captaincy of the Pune team. No fans protested. I am sure people would have protested if Dhoni were dropped as captain of India. Captains are changed midway through the IPL. A captain has to make way and become a substitute player if the combination doesn't work, as happened with a great like Ricky Ponting at Mumbai Indians.

This simple lesson in multiple capabilities is something we can apply in life and the corporate world. A single-skill cricketer does not have a role in the IPL team, however good he is at the international level. The best Test batsmen who cannot adapt to T20 don't get picked, but the best bowler still has a chance. Teams tend to pick players with multiple skills—batting, bowling, fielding, wicket-keeping, captaincy. So these days, we need to have more capabilities in life and at the workplace as compared to the past.

Equally, one needs to adapt to a new world. One cannot play Test cricket and expect to succeed in a fast-changing world. This is a challenge for many managers past their prime. They are all digital immigrants and just don't have a sense of how to work in a digital world. Rahane and Pujara in cricket are examples.

One has to constantly re-evaluate the capability set and be future-ready in life.

Shopping Mall Model

The third approach I want people to think about in managing their life and career is what I call the shopping mall model. This applies to managers in start-up companies. To be fair, this model has been used before in advertising, market research, journalism and consumer electronics, where people tend to move from one door to the next, as in a shopping mall.

Professionals tend to shop around for jobs as one shops around in a shopping mall. This approach is relevant as long as you have relevant experience and have produced worthwhile results. But the shopping mall approach to a career doesn't work beyond the middle-management stage.

* * *

Life needs some skill sets. These also help immensely in a career.

The first is time management.

Time management is a top capability you need in managing yourself. Half the impression you create as a professional comes from the way you manage time and manage deadlines. I have seen both outstanding time managers and poor time managers. I have always found that good time managers set higher standards for themselves and for people who work for them. People who manage time well never seem stretched for time and never offer the excuse of being busy. They seem to have the time for many things. When one is a poor time manager, one has to compensate for that with good social skills, so that people are not upset with or angry at you. Poor time management shows an inability to empathize with the other person's priorities.

The second is emotions and insecurities.

Managing emotions is important. People in the corridor normally ask about the boss's mood because of the fluctuating emotions that the boss displays in a day. People want to catch the boss in a good mood as opposed to in a bad mood.

Managing insecurities will be big in the coming decade. FOMO (fear of missing out) is the new insecurity in town, especially among the Gen Z. A social media-driven world, rapid progress in some sectors and luck will combine to make you feel insecure vis-à-vis your peer group or the people you know. There is no antidote to insecurity. I have seen that senior managers are more insecure today than they were, say, ten years ago, because the standards expected and the demands made of them are growing. Managers who are insecure of their subordinates' talent or of other people in the firm are growing. This hinders the building of friendships at the workplace, and leads to politics and stress. Even if you are confident, you need to manage the insecurities of your peer group or even of your boss. How subtly you handle that will determine your continued success.

The third is ambition.

Everyone is ambitious—some are so in a more in-your-face way than the others. I worked for a few people who would always keep bragging about their old achievements decades down the line. Ambition is good, as it propels progress and raises the bar. But when ambition becomes purely self-centred, the person and the organization are in trouble. One of the companies I worked for had a bunch of super-ambitious people, but that company came to be known for poor teamwork and lost respect among industry colleagues. The company suffered, and many of the overambitious characters didn't realize their ambitions.

The fourth is relationships.

Managing your relationship with the organization is important, as it determines how people perceive you as an organization man/woman or as a bystander. The relationship between you and the organization should be one of pride, else you should not be working in that organization. This is much like the pride a soldier has in working to protect the country. If there is no sense of pride, then it will show in many slippages at work and also in your communication. Whatever you do, do not run down your organization at any external forum.

Teams will be different this decade. Managing a team is going to be very different over the next decade, with hybrid working, etc. A good leader needs to be fair in judging the contribution of his team members. A good leader will not create an inner circle of people who come physically to work and an outer circle of those working in a hybrid manner.

Judging a team member on the basis of their impact and contribution will become more important. Leaders will need to communicate significantly better in a digital world.

Managing a business is never easy, and it will get more difficult in the coming years. Managing a business in tough and turbulent times will be a challenge. Because of digital business models, I think value in every industry will be destroyed in the short run, before it turns positive over time. India has 1.8 million companies registered with the Ministry of Corporate Affairs. In 2019, 30 per cent of these companies, or 6,80,000 companies, closed down, either because of poor performance or because of non-compliance with regulatory filings.

A leader needs to rethink the capabilities needed for business competitiveness and also pivot the company to a digital model—be it omnichannel or a new digital business model. This is a challenge for leaders who come from a physical world as opposed to the digital natives in the organization.

'Agility' will be a buzzword this decade, and every industry will have to become speedier, in terms of addressing the change in consumer/customer needs and in terms of going to market.

Agility in an organization will come from using technology and pushing horizontal collaboration. This is against the grain of those organizations that have been a collection of vertical hierarchies. The leader of the next decade will push for significant fluidity in structures.

This book has a collection of views, thoughts and experiences of outstanding professionals in various fields, and touches on the subjects of managing oneself, managing the team and managing the business. My intent is to enable you to learn from the various professionals and build your own pathway to your destination.

I think it's appropriate and fitting that Sachin Tendulkar has written the foreword to this book. Sachin is quintessentially Indian but recognized and revered around the globe. He is one of India's biggest brands on the global stage. He is a great example of staying the course, for over twenty-four years, at the top level, of reinventing oneself, of leading a team, of supporting a team and of being a thought leader in areas even outside cricket. His discipline and commitment to his craft and whatever he does are unmatched. Sachin is the best example I could think of managing yourself, your team and your business.

I researched the idea for this book with consumers, who gave it a high five. I also researched various book cover designs before picking this winner.

Enjoy the book!

March 2022   Shiv Shivakumar
Mumbai

Section I

Managing Yourself

'You have no control over where you started—your family, your location, etc., but you should have a good sense of where you want to end. That's in your hands.'

Your journey is an outcome of the choices you make. Some choices are in your control, some are not in your control. I argue that you should be good at things that are under your control, and that will make a big difference to your journey.

You could well think: What are the things under my control? The following are fully in your control:

a. Managing your time
b. Managing your ambition
c. Managing your learning
d. Managing your energy
e. Managing your relationship with your organization

Let me take you through my observations in each of these areas in the subsequent pages.

Managing Your Time

Time is one element all of us have the same quantity of—some make the hour work for them and some waste the hour. Time is very cultural, and the attitude to time is culture-dependent.

The hybrid model of working and interaction with colleagues and the ecosystem will place a premium on how you manage time this decade. As colleagues we do not like dealing with people who are tardy, who continuously miss deadlines, who need constant reminding, people who do not reply to messages or emails.

There are two ways of managing time:

1. On-time
2. Flexi-time

On-time people and cultures are well organized. On-time people see time as linear. They manage their calendars, and once a time is given, very rarely do they need reminders or rarely do they postpone the event. Countries which are on-time are the USA, Denmark, Switzerland, Germany, Japan and the UK. In the US, Japan and Switzerland, coming on time is late.

Cities which have an on-time reputation are Mumbai, Hong Kong, London, New York and Geneva. In many of these cities, time is money, and everyone works to a schedule—the system places a premium on time and these cities monetize time as a variable.

Six Most Punctual Nations in the World

COUNTRY	FACTS ABOUT TIME IN EACH COUNTRY
Switzerland	Switzerland is the world's watchmaking capital. The Swiss are also known for precision, so it's no wonder they are always on time! Coffee shops in Swiss cities tend to be crowded at 4 p.m. every day because everybody takes their coffee breaks at this hour.
Denmark	The World Clock in Copenhagen began keeping time in 1955 and is expected to accurately keep time for the next 5,70,000 years!
Japan	The average annual delay of the Shinkansen bullet trains is thirty-six seconds!
Germany	Do NOT arrive late when invited for dinner. The host will consider this extremely rude.
The Netherlands	Dutch children are taught how to create schedules as early as primary school. To them, everything must be according to schedule, including work, meals and recreational activities.
South Korea	Restaurants will not accept customers an hour before they close.

Source: https://www.philstar.com/lifestyle/business-life/2019/04/06/1911911/6-most-punctual-nations-world

The Shinkansen bullet train in Japan has an average delay of less than twenty seconds every year. That's mind-blowing as a measure. If the train is late, the train driver/conductor bows and apologizes to every passenger. There was an unheard-of situation when a bullet train in Japan left thirty seconds before scheduled departure time, and the train company profusely apologized to everyone.

Ratio of Late Deliveries among Seven Top Countries

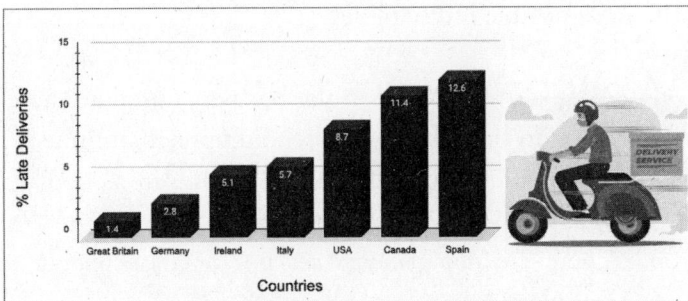

Image source: https://www.freepik.com/
Source: https://www.bringg.com/blog/delivery/punctual-countries-demand-world/

Flexi-time cultures view time as being fluid. Time in these cultures is event- and person-dependent. Being late is forgivable in these cultures. A lot of African and Asian countries, including India, fall into this bracket.

In 1959, anthropologist Edward Hall described cultural rules of 'time' as 'the silent language' in his book of the same title. According to Hall, time conveys clearer messages than words. In many of these cultures time is a socio-economic status marker.

In these countries, it is common to thank the chief guest or guest of honour for sparing time from his/her busy schedule repeatedly in every speech made at an event. In high-power-distance cultures, people of higher status are always late, and it's a privilege for people to get an audience with them.

Even in similar cultures, rituals and their practice can vary. The time of marriage in a south Indian wedding is sacrosanct and based on a 'mahurat', while the marriage time in a north Indian wedding is variable.

Just look around in any company, and you will see some of the signs of time indiscipline:

1. All goals to be filled in the business portal are never done on time; HR teams send umpteen reminders.
2. All appraisals are not done on time; in some cases appraisals are not done, period.
3. There are departments set up to chase people to complete tasks and processes.

4. All notes on customer visits or system-partner visits are not circulated, and nor is there a database in a OneNote or an equivalent system.

We tend to classify people who are excellent time managers or chasers as 'hyper' individuals.

Let's now look at some possible reasons why some people manage time poorly:

1. The first reason is that some people can never say no. They keep asking for more work; they are not able to prioritize or even understand what the work entails. Being busy is a 'badge' for such people.

The Power of 'No'

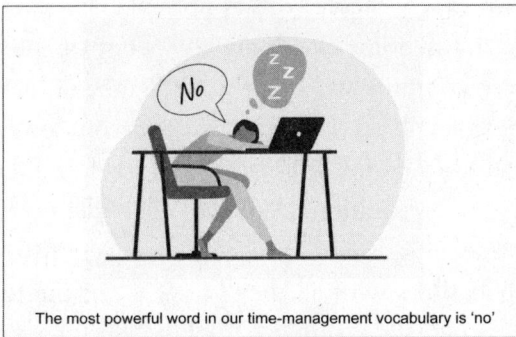

The most powerful word in our time-management vocabulary is 'no'

Image source: https://www.freepik.com/
Source: https://www.dovico.com/blog/2018/03/06/time-management-facts-figures/

2. Some people are perfectionists—they always want the presentation or job or response or anything to be 110 per cent right, and hence end up wasting time. In tomorrow's world, with more information and

more forgetting, this perfectionism will be a sin. A good example in a company is the annual planning process. Companies waste far too much time on many things they don't control and still want a point of view on.

3. Procrastination. Some people procrastinate like mad. A series of twenty questions for every aspect . . . What if X happens? What if Y says so? What if they don't accept? A series of what-ifs. I am not saying don't ask questions, but just keeping on asking the same questions endlessly gets you nothing of value.

4. Lack of empathy. Some people don't empathize with what others go through when you keep them hanging around or don't have time for them. In many Eastern cultures, we accept this as normal.

5. Laziness. Some people are lazy. They can only do one task at a time and don't want to take on more. Such people talk up their work, so that you don't find out that they do little. They expand work to fill time.

6. Poor preparation. We see this all the time in presentations and speeches. Managers tend to pack their slides with all they know about the topic, and hence a slide ends up looking like a pasta bowl. Worse, managers will want to read every line and explain. My way of making slides is to have a visual and a maximum of twenty-four words per slide. The narrative is more important than what's on the slide. I typically take 2–3 minutes per slide, and if I have a twenty-minute presentation, I will go in with a

maximum of 6–10 slides. Preparing speaker notes and running through the slides will help you manage time better in any presentation. One can easily make out people who come ill-prepared or unprepared for meetings. This is a drain on everyone's time, because everyone is required to go through the basics when they could have been driving higher-order conversations leading to decisions.

7. Lack of follow-up. Some people don't know how to follow up with others who have to do their jobs in order for the former to complete their job. Sometimes work happens in series in an organization, and lack of follow-up makes people poor time managers when it comes to their work. One has to know when to follow up with peers and bosses in order to get your work done on time.

8. Habit of postponing. Some people just postpone work. They tend to move simple, everyday parts of a job unnecessarily to the next day or week. Closing work or closing parts of a job that can be completed today actually help you close more aspects of your job. So don't postpone to tomorrow what you can complete today.

9. Lack of job-chain awareness. Managers do not recognize how their work and job add up to a larger picture, and hence they don't see completing their work on time as an important element to the chain of work.

10. Plain time-wasting. Many managers waste time at work. They spend a lot of time idling, gossiping,

walking around the office and drinking endless cups of tea/coffee with anyone who is available. Social media is actually a big time-wasting distraction at work. Some managers spend more time on social media than on their company agenda.

Let me now turn to good time managers and what they do well to make time management a 'super habit'. I have been lucky to see some really good time managers, like R. Gopalakrishnan of Unilever and Tata Sons, Olli-Pekka at Nokia and Indra Nooyi at PepsiCo.

Time Management: Interesting Facts and Figures

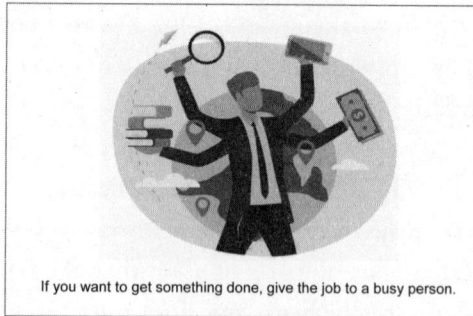

If you want to get something done, give the job to a busy person.

Image source: https://www.freepik.com/
Source: https://www.dovico.com/blog/2018/03/06/time-management-facts-figures/

I pick my lessons from people who manage time well, and the lessons are:

1. They are organized in everything they do, they maintain a calendar, they stick to a calendar, they rarely cancel meetings, and if they do, they give you

an alternative time slot. So run a proper calendar is my first tip.

2. Good time managers come fully prepared for meetings. We spend more than 25 per cent of a day in meetings. These are places to move work, to brief about work and to take decisions. Being well prepared for every meeting is a gift you can give to your organization and team.

3. They make copious notes, and the notes help them develop a good memory for subsequent meetings. Good time managers maintain journals like nobody else, and this gives them a huge advantage.

4. They delegate what can be delegated effectively.

5. They follow through on promises they have made personally or on behalf of their team.

6. Good time managers prioritize when they see a conflict; they make a choice.

7. They know when to multitask and when to avoid multitasking. It's better to avoid multitasking when your full attention is needed on a topic for discussion. The cellphone and messages in a cellphone are the biggest distractions for multitaskers. So, keep the phone aside in important meetings and discussions.

8. They have regular breaks in their schedule, either to stretch their legs, to get a cup of tea/coffee or to return missed calls.

9. They always respond. They respond to emails, messages and return all their missed calls.

10. They believe that time management is a multi-way benefit system. If they manage time well, they can

influence the system and manage it better, and hence good time management has multiple benefits overall.

Plan Better and Save Time

One hour of planning will save ten hours of doing.

Image source: https://www.freepik.com/
Source: https://www.dovico.com/blog/2018/03/06/time-management-facts-figures/

Managing Your Ambition

I want to start by saying that ambition is good. Ambition propels individuals, teams, companies and society to do better. Ambition starts with some desire to achieve something, but more important is the tenacity to work towards achieving it. Ambition does not have entitlement built into it ever. Everyone aspires to be something, but they might not have the ambition to go for it. So, please make that clear distinction between what you want and what you are willing to do or not do to get there.

Ambition doesn't have a 'safe', well-understood definition in any company. There are some professions where ambition is on steroids, like stock market trading, investment banking, journalism, car racing. There are other industries or professions where you don't want to see super ambition, like in doctors, in policemen, in guardians of the law, etc.

It is fair to say that all companies want ambitious employees, which simply means that companies want tasks, challenges and work completed ahead of time in order to benefit the company agenda. Companies tend to equate high-productive employees with ambition and vice versa.

Ambition that is unchecked can lead to catastrophic results, as in the case of Enron, Barings and a few start-ups. Aristotle is believed to have said that men's ambition is the root cause of many an injustice.

I have seen that excessive ambition damages careers and relationships at work, and leads to failure. I have seen a few of my peers who were unbearable at work, who blatantly wore their ambition on their sleeves and who would run down their peer group at the drop of a hat. I am glad that a number of them didn't make it to CEO roles, as that would have been a wrong template for a successful leader in any company.

What could ambition be in an uncertain world of tomorrow, where there are no clear paths and no easy answers? I think ambition must be more tempered in tomorrow's world, since fast success and fast failure will happen in cycles and in double-quick time.

Individuals are ambitious, as also companies. If you were to talk to the consumer electronics trade partners in India, they would tell you that Samsung and LG are aggressive and ambitious to a fault. It is interesting that these trade partners like the money they make on these companies but are uncertain about their trust in the companies because of this nature of ambition and aggression.

Ambition: Interesting Facts and Figures

In Japan, if someone is too outwardly ambitious, their colleagues won't work with them. One of the most famous Japanese proverbs is, 'The nail that sticks out, gets hammered down.'

Image source: https://www.freepik.com/
Source: https://www.bbc.com/worklife/article/20140805-ambition-born-or-bred

People find it difficult to trust an ambitious person, because they feel that such a person will use them as a pawn on their journey.

Leaders play a role in driving ambition in an individual and a team. How many times we hear leaders tell people, 'You have done it in the past. We have done it. Let's do it again.' This kind of exhortation works, but within limits.

I think that well-balanced ambition is good for both individuals and companies. Well-balanced ambition leads to creativity and innovation, higher productivity, better teamwork and better work satisfaction.

Well-balanced ambition is about placing the ambition for the company or the team ahead of personal ambition; it's about getting to growth via learning and building capabilities as opposed to empty slogans; it's about being wide-eyed about success and not turning a blind eye to failure or brushing failure under the carpet.

Ambition, in some cases, comes from fierce determination between the ears—i.e., in the head. The New Zealand cricket team is always an understated but overperforming team, with low overt ambition. The All Blacks, the New Zealand rugby team, is the opposite—it's a very successful team that tries and whittles down the opponents' morale with their haka, a traditional dance of the Māori people, before every game. Both work!

One needs to think of some capabilities when one charts an ambitious path. Time in job tends to kill ambition as the manager/leader tends to rely on what's worked as opposed to trying new things and setting new ambition.

I think ambition will need you to rethink your technical and personal development goals. You cannot achieve your ambitious targets if you don't develop a new edge.

Collectivistic Cultures That Frown upon Ambition

01 India	13 Brazil	25 Lebanon	37 Zambia
02 Pakistan	14 Ethiopia	26 Portugal	38 Kenya
03 Bangladesh	15 Bulgaria	27 Romania	39 Uganda
04 Indonesia	16 Guatemala	28 Russia	40 Somalia
05 Iraq	17 Dominican R	29 Ukraine	41 Poland
06 Afghanistan	18 El Salvador	30 Saudi Arabia	42 Philippines
07 Cyprus	19 Mexico	31 Serbia	43 Japan
08 Ghana	20 Georgia	32 Singapore	44 Sri Lanka
09 Nepal	21 Kazakhstan	33 Spain	45 Azerbaijan
10 Argentina	22 Morocco	34 Turkey	46 Polynesia
11 Armenia	23 Myanmar	35 Vietnam	47 Greece
12 Belarus	24 Korea	36 Nigeria	48 Cuba

Source: https://psychology.fandom.com/wiki/Collectivist_and_individualist_cultures

Individualistic Cultures That Celebrate Ambition

01	USA		13	Germany
02	Australia		14	South Africa
03	UK		15	Luxembourg
04	Canada		16	Guatemala
05	Netherlands		17	Czech R
06	Italy		18	Austria
07	Hungary		19	Israel
08	New Zealand		20	Slovakia
09	France		21	Poland
10	Belgium		22	Lithuania
11	Ireland		23	Latvia
12	Switzerland		24	Estonia

Source: https://psychology.fandom.com/wiki/Collectivist_and_individualist_cultures

Successful people experience bouts of ambition; they feed on that to ride the wave and go to the next level.

One thing I have learnt is that ambition is innate—you cannot teach someone to be ambitious.

Watch out for the following when you think of your ambition.

Too much ambition is seen when:

1. There is a thin line dividing ambition and personal glory.
2. There is contempt for the past and the legacy of the predecessor in the job.
3. There is excessive focus on tasks and low emphasis on people.
4. There is a frantic pace of work.
5. One observes a sense of entitlement.

6. There is petty jealousy at work
7. The results are way off the mark in relation to the promises made.

Too little ambition is evident when you see:

1. People are unsure of what they want to achieve.
2. People seem bored in their roles.
3. There is a misfit between capability in individual and capability in a team.
4. People struggling with understanding what it takes to get ahead in a company.
5. People being in their comfort zone.

Managing Your Learning

The world is changing so quickly in so many areas, and there is so much information available in the public domain now. If one does not learn quickly, then one will be termed 'educated unemployed' or 'educated but living in the past'. Lack of access is not a barrier to learning any more.

In many countries, learning is a process that helps one secure some marks and get a degree or a certificate. Marks are a measure of intelligence, but that's an outdated concept in a future world. True learning is about thinking about each concept, its application, trying variations of the concept in your mind to see what is possible.

Workplace learning is very different. There are no marks there, except class-participation marks in a meeting and the marks/stripes you get when your concept is accepted and executed to deliver results. So, workplace learning has much more trial and error built into it, as opposed to the traditional learning which everyone goes through.

I have seen professionals ride on the coattails of their degrees, which were completed in a very different world. I believe there is no such thing as good or bad learning, as long as you learn and know how to apply it correctly.

There are various approaches to learning:

1. Self-learning: I have seen people pick up a book or a bunch of books, go speak to experts, watch videos on a topic, etc. This type of learning requires focus; it requires you to take time out, understand what you need to learn and then evaluate learning in your own way. This is self-development at its best. Self-learning people are curious. According to a *Harvard Business Review* analysis, curious people at work are 34 per cent more creative.

2. Learning by watching others: This is something we do innately at work. We watch the way the boss presents his ideas, we watch the way someone answers questions in a press conference, we watch the mannerisms of people, we copy the ones we think are worth it and junk the ones that we don't like. We watch the way people conduct themselves in formal and informal situations, we watch the way people dress. This is possibly the most normal form of learning at work.

Time Spent for Learning – Be An Expert!

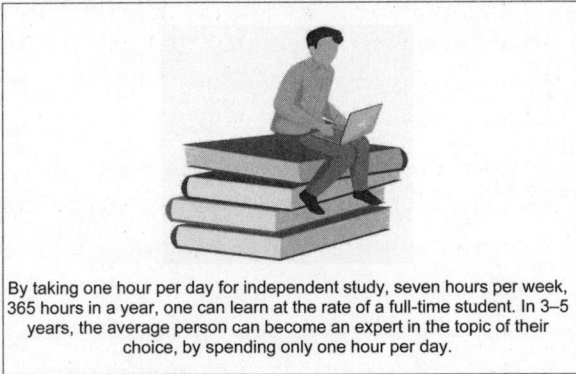

By taking one hour per day for independent study, seven hours per week, 365 hours in a year, one can learn at the rate of a full-time student. In 3–5 years, the average person can become an expert in the topic of their choice, by spending only one hour per day.

Image source: https://www.freepik.com/
Source: https://www.dovico.com/blog/2018/03/06/time-management-facts-figures/

3. Learning by doing, aka experiential learning: This is a theory of education postulated by American philosopher John Dewey. He applied this at the University of Chicago. It is based on the philosophy that we learn more about something when we actually 'do' it. We apply concepts at work, we try new processes, new methods of dealing with people, we try new ways to create value for customers and ecosystem partners. In this method we tend to vary the variables we value and tweak them to achieve the desired results. There are simple life examples: we learnt swimming by doing, we learnt to ride a bicycle by doing, we learnt to drive a car by doing, and we learnt how the experience works and doesn't work for us. In tomorrow's world, we can try a lot more things at work because tests can be done either with

a design for one or a design for a billion. Technology allows us to experience learning differently. So I would encourage you to test, test and test again to learn.

4. Learning by attending courses: This is standard practice in most organizations where there are a number of courses offered by internal and external faculty. I see that people want to go to a training course if it's an exotic location or there is rockstar faculty or there are a number of their close friends attending the course. If these conditions don't exist, then people keep dropping off courses at the last minute. In my career, if someone was nominated for a course, I would never allow the person to withdraw despite various requests from his/her weak bosses to let the person skip the course for some urgent work that needed to be done. This last-minute withdrawal sets the wrong tone in an organization about learning. My advice to you: courses are not junkets; if you treat them like that, you will learn little.

5. Learning by being part of project teams: I have found great value in this method of learning. Project teams have a definite scope of work, a definite work plan and members who can add value to each other. This is the closest to getting multidisciplinary learning quickly. In my career, I have been a part of the low unit price strategy team, emerging markets project team, Africa project team, guaranteed volume project team, reworking HUL value proposition

on campus team, etc. I learnt from even the junior-most members in the team, because they had very unique and varied points of view. I would urge you to get into project teams on every topic you are interested in and cannot find enough resources to experiment with. This also happens when you hire a consulting firm, and the firm builds various streams of work involving employees. Do volunteer for such projects, as this is the lowest-risk method in terms of learning.

My recipe for you: one can learn by reading books, one can learn by talking to at least two people outside your industry every month, one can learn by following trends. I look at trends as those that impact the individual, the family and society. If a trend impacts all three, you can be sure that it will be big, like mobile telephony, diabetes, food delivery services, ride sharing, EVs. One can learn by bouncing ideas off people you trust.

Another method I use is to learn by teaching. You have to be good if you want to teach a concept. This is what I call a 'teachable point of view'. Teaching helps you refine your point of view with examples; it helps you reflect on your experience with the concept and on how your view has changed over the years. So a good way to be a great learner is to be a great teacher. The first place you can start teaching is your alma mater and your company, or with your own team. Teaching and learning, both make you relevant in a fast-paced world.

Managing Your Energy

There is a new school of thought that says managing energy is more important than time. This school argues that time is finite and should not be allocated equally to all tasks, that it should be allocated the way your energy flows, i.e., reserve the best energy for the most important tasks.

I differ from this view. I believe both are important, I feel that you cannot manage your energy and prioritization if you don't manage time well. So, managing time well is the starting point to managing your energy.

Energy is about physical, mental, emotional and spiritual energy. Managers tend to bring the first three to work every day, but the spiritual part is something that I have not seen normally at work.

All of us want to start strong on any task or work assigned to us. The trick is to stay strong and finish strong. That needs management of energy. You get energy when different elements come together—being physically fit; eating the right food and the right amount of it; getting enough sleep; having enough rest time or rest breaks; and using a holiday or a weekend to recharge the batteries.

Let's look at a few examples of how some successful people manage energy.

Warren Buffett has days where he has no meetings or engagements. He uses these days to recharge himself and to think about the future.

Kamala Harris, the vice president of the USA, exercises every morning to get energy and focus going for the day.

Jeff Bezos of Amazon starts his day at 10 a.m. every day. He uses the morning to energize himself for the tasks to follow.

A recent article mentioned that Lionel Messi, the famous Argentine footballer, walks 83 per cent in the course of a match and really runs and focuses in the balance 17 per cent, when he scores all those goals or assists the scoring of a goal. The work equivalent of this is managers who have no papers on their table, appear to be idle, but get the work done.

Some managers try meditation every morning to give themselves a sense of peace and comfort for the energy required through the day.

I think the modern manager has too many distractions, and if you have to manage your energy, you need to minimize distractions. You cannot work, party, drink and still hope to have high energy. The concept of work hard and play harder is valid for a day, at best for a week; it cannot work in the long run—something has to give, and that will be your health.

In the last decade we managed energy to be more productive; in the next decade we will manage energy to have a more fulfilling life.

So, how does one manage energy?

1. You need to recognize what's important and what's unimportant. Placing more time on unimportant events will dissipate your energy.
2. There is a time for work, there is a time to recoup, and there's a time to expend energy partying or whatever. Excess of anything on that list will make

you lose energy and focus. I see people using their weekends to travel, party, play sports, and then they land up at work on Monday morning fully drained. Is that really good management of energy?

3. Early-morning routines are good energy-builders, be it walking, jogging, cycling. Build some early-morning routine so that you look forward to it every night.

4. The commute to work can be energy-sapping in cities like Mumbai, Hong Kong, London, New York, etc. I know people in my team who travel ninety minutes each way to work, and I just feel bad for them. How you manage your energy through that sapping ride is crucial for the way you start work. Some people do carpooling, some find something to read—each person has a way of managing this tedious and monotonous aspect of work. The hybrid model of the future will help these employees.

5. The best energy comes from doing good work—it feeds into itself. The average employee gets energy from his/her boss and colleagues at work. Employees get a high when the boss addresses them by name in the morning or acknowledges their presence in a meeting or makes small talk with them. Employees get energy when they know they have a meeting with the boss. I feel many leaders underestimate their role in building energy at the workplace. This is very true in offices spread over different floors. Employees get energized to see their CEO on their

floor, at their desk. They feel this gives them an opportunity to showcase their work or tell him/her something important. I have seen many CEOs closet themselves in their cabins—they are not accessible to anyone beyond their management team. I used to make it a habit to walk every floor every day I was in office, and I would try and have lunch with different sets of employees. This gave me a good and fresh perspective to what was going on in the company. Team colleagues can play an important role in providing energy, much like teammates in sports encourage and energize each other during a game. Here's an old psychological tale from cricket. At the height of their domination of cricket, the West Indies cricket team systematically targeted the opposition captain to ensure that he didn't succeed. This, the West Indies achieved 90 per cent of the time. The opposition team was demoralized and was never energized by their underperforming captain. The same is true at work—employees cannot be energized by cynical, underperforming leaders.

6. Energy is generated in organizations via rituals, like monthly dinners, lunches, offsites, monthly awards, recognition, etc. It is important to keep these positive and not let them become a crib session against the boss or the company.

7. Energy also comes from doing tasks effortlessly. It is a fact that when we get good at something, we tend to do it better and faster.

8. Always expend your energy on the big tasks, the important tasks every morning. That's a good way to start and also to get your mojo for the day.

9. I have seen many managers re-energize via music, via sport or via a break. Young employees seem to work better as the day goes on—it's something of a continuation of college life.

10. Facilities at work make a difference. I visited the Meta office in Menlo Park in 2018. The complex has many restaurants offering different cuisines as well as a laundry service—it's like an upscale college dormitory. And I saw employees working everywhere. There was a palpable sense of energy on that campus. Young mothers in PepsiCo India were energized when we put in a crèche in the office. We had taken a big worry off their list.

Manage Your Relationship with the Organization

I believe that the relationship between an employee and his organization must be one of pride. Is this always possible? Maybe not. If you are not proud of working for the organization and its associated benefits or pitfalls, then you must leave. There is no point in staying in an organization and turning negative or cynical.

There is no measure or metric to judge your relationship with the organization. The whole thing is qualitative.

A decade ago, James Allen and Chris Zook of Bain Consulting talked of the concept of ownership and urged organizations to develop the owner's mindset in every employee. This comes from a compelling vision, a clear purpose, a distaste for bureaucracy and a strong commitment to the success of the company. The owner's mindset comes from an obsession with the front line where customer meetings happen.

Interesting Fact

At Red Bull, employees are encouraged to come up with ideas themselves. If an idea is a good one, the employee concerned is given (alone or with others) the freedom to really develop it and put it into practice.

Doing so gives employees a great sense of responsibility and they also become the owner of their own promotion or event.

Image source: https://www.freepik.com/
Source: https://www.effectory.com/knowledge/how-to-increase-employee-commitment/

Young companies should have a natural advantage on each of these parameters. The start-up ecosystem should think about this. When start-ups grow, they reach what Allen and Zook call a stall out, where growth begins to slow and a stifling atmosphere sets in.

What employees value in their employers keeps changing. Every employee wants to be paid more, but that doesn't mean that employees in high-paying organizations are happy and have a better relationship with their organizations. Money is necessary but not a sufficient condition for pride in a company. If a company does not provide adequate money, then it has to balance on many other drag parameters—like poor consequence management of poor performance, no hire-and-fire culture, acceptance of low standards at work. Companies do this because they believe a known devil is better than an unknown angel, and they believe that they cannot attract good talent.

Source: https://www.effectory.com/knowledge/how-to-increase-employee-commitment/

For an employee, pride in an organization comes from many aspects:

1. It comes from storytelling: tales of valour, tales of beating the odds, of what the company faced and how it addressed the challenges and came out of it. In Hindustan Unilever, there were enough stories about government price control and how the company managed to survive. In Nokia, there were many

stories about how Nokia beat Motorola in so many of its big markets.

2. It comes from senior managers' behaviour in the organization. If senior managers are inspiring, communicative and visible, then employees feel a sense of pride working for them and hence for the company.

3. Pride comes from the commitment the organization has to society. A lot of Tata and Aditya Birla Group employees take pride in their organization's higher commitment to nation-building. Soldiers of the Indian armed forces take pride in what the armed forces do for the country.

4. It comes from consistency of policy and fairness in applying policy. Employees do not mind tough policies as long as they are implemented honestly and fairly. Employees lose faith and hence pride in an organization that makes too many exceptions. I worked for such an organization where exceptions were expected at every level, and I had to change a lot of things to bring a sense of rigour to the application of policies.

5. I think smaller teams have a higher sense of commitment and alignment with the overall organization versus larger teams. In larger teams, everyone assumes that it is someone else's job to build that pride.

6. It comes from a mindset where the employee feels that the organization values different talents and is adding value to his/her CV.

7. It comes when employees and senior managers treat the organization's money respectfully and do not waste it. When leaders and senior managers waste the organization's money, it has short-term excitement but doesn't build long-term pride. At one of the companies I worked in, there was a standard gift that was given in every conference. I stopped that practice because I felt that we had to focus on what the conference offered rather than on the gift. A loss-making company cannot keep giving gifts. When a loss-making company keeps giving lollies, it's difficult to build a sense of cost-consciousness in the team. My head of sales couldn't understand this basic logic. I always maintain that you should treat company money more respectfully than you treat your own money.

8. It comes when there is low double-speak, and it comes when the values of the organization are practised by senior managers. Let me give you the best example for what is not practised. Every company I have worked for has at some point had a 'One' approach, where everyone in different companies and SBUs were expected to sink their differences and work towards a common goal of One goodness. This is farthest from the truth, as the One approach hurts the very empires and power structures that managers have built, and they see it as a threat. I haven't seen One structures and systems work without the CEO breaking a few eggs.

9. Pride in organization comes if confidential information is kept confidential, and there is no loose talk.

10. It comes when the industry recognizes and awards the organization for good work. Every employee feels good when their company is lauded as an exemplar of industry best practice in that field. This leads to pride and hence more commitment for even better work.

Employees see all this every day, and then they decide if they are proud of their association. It is for both leaders and employees to build this pride. Pride-building is not the HR's role and task; it is the everyday job of senior managers.

General V.P. Malik

General Malik is one of India's celebrated and cerebral generals. He was the Kargil war general and led the forces from the front. General Malik was the nineteenth chief of the army staff and led the army from 30 September 1997 to 30 September 2000. He has been awarded the Ati Vishisht Seva Medal and the Param Vishisht Seva Medal. He is also the author of two books. General Malik is an independent director on many multinational boards. In this interview he talks about his formative years, leadership, moving cities with transfers, staying fit and the importance of being where the action is.

You are one of India's most famous generals. Please tell us how this journey started. How did you choose to go to the National Defence Academy (NDA) ahead of the other options that you might have had at that point?

I was born in Dera Ismail Khan, a military cantonment on the western side of the Indus River. My father left his business and joined the army in 1942. I had some other relations in the services too. In 1954, I was studying at the Delhi Polytechnic School. I found it hard to cope with physics and maths. A career in the armed forces looked socially attractive and suited my aspirations.

In school, I was quite okay as far as sports and physical training were concerned. The basic problem I faced was that I had to travel by bus to the school, and it took me one and a half hours for each trip. It was very tiring. And maybe that was why I lost interest in studies. But I was always fond of adventure. Although I will not say I was physically strong, I was all right in sports. And I had good general knowledge. In those days we used to have general knowledge tests, in which I did well. That helped me get through the NDA.

Going from a second lieutenant to the nineteenth chief of the army staff is no easy task. How did you manage this journey? What were your personal learnings?

During training, a lot of emphasis was laid on military discipline, character-building, integrity, moral courage, military ethics, values, ethos and pride, teamwork and camaraderie, hard work, physical fitness, sense of adventure, military history and to some extent general awareness. But the most important learning and part of the journey/experience had to do with leadership-building. This included all aspects of dealing with human capital, e.g., fairness, diversity, plurality, empowerment, dedication to duty, with passion and dynamism.

Leadership training and experience in the army can be divided into three parts:

- Junior level: Discipline, basic knowledge, physical fitness, self-pride, daring and, most importantly, team spirit.
- Middle level: Confidence, more knowledge, communication and analytical skills, audacity, adaptability and ability to delegate.
- Senior level: Vision, intuition, anticipating change, collaboration, calmness, ethical values and resilience.

I did quite well in my professional studies and assessable courses throughout my career, and never got overlooked in terms of career advancement.

But I had challenging command assignments throughout my career, from the major to lieutenant general rank.

Disappointments:

- Inability to get adequate funds, to make up for the deficiencies in weapons and equipment, and to carry out the much-needed modernization.
- Life in the armed forces was a self-contained life. So there was a lack of exposure to Indian arts and culture, also to the mainstream socio-economic and socio-political environment.
- Missing the growing-up years of my children.

You had a transferable job, sir. When people change cities, or anticipate further moves from one area to another, especially for work reasons, they are reluctant to involve themselves deeply in friendships. That is because they want to avoid any pain of separation later. As a result, their social circle mostly consists of work associations. Was that true in your case as well?

You know, ours is a slightly different way of life. The separation from within the family of the husband being posted in field area, and the wife staying in a peace area—this was the norm in those days. Every few years you went to a field area, where you spent two or three years. The wife accepted it, and we would come on leave, and be with the wife and children. And it was kind of accepted. I would say that it made the family pretty strong. You know, the wife learnt—whether it was driving or taking the children to school, and you know, facing all the hardships when she's alone. But of course, as a father, you missed out on the growing-up stage of your children. During my posting in Mizoram, in 1968–69, I used to get a letter from my wife, every twenty or twenty-five days. And that was the time when my son—my first child—was born. And so after that, the same kind of habit [writing letters] continued when my daughter was born. My wife would make them write a few lines on a sheet of paper, and she would post them to me. Then, of course, subsequently the telephones and all came up, and the letters became fewer. I won't say they stopped, but they became fewer.

Making friends was not so difficult, because you were in a cantonment area, where you have a number of people living the same kind of life. As far as the adaptability in civil life is concerned, in those days, when I became a brigadier general, I also got a lot of complaints from the ladies who said that because they had to shift so often, the education of their children suffered. They used to complain about the children having to shift schools, you know, every few years.

Later in life, I once attended a placement event at the Symbiosis College in Pune. So I went there as a senior officer at that time. And I asked the people from the HR department: 'Why do you people go around looking for the children of army officers?' And they said that they find them to be very adaptable, because army children keep moving from station to station. They don't mind going to any station, and they make friends very easily. So that is a plus point, which not many of us want to see. One of the reasons why our children are doing well in civil life is their adaptability.

It is critical to be physically healthy in order to be mentally fit. You are mentally sharp even today. What has been your health regimen through the years?

I have always been health-conscious and have the ability to lead the troops from the front (for as long as possible) and to participate in troop-level activities, including troop-level sports. I played soccer and squash in my younger days, and now golf. I love walking.

You had a very hectic schedule. How did you maintain your energy levels?

I think a lot comes from discipline. I always say that discipline is not so much about saluting the flag and saying *saavdhan*. Discipline in the army has taught me how to sequence your work, without wasting time. So you look at your engagements sequentially. If I have to have an interview with you, I should ask myself how much time do I have for preparation, keeping in view my other engagements, etc. So you plan your activities that way. And I consider that as a part of discipline.

People in corporate houses often complain that they do not get time to invest in fitness, and some of these problems are indeed real, in the sense that most of their time is demanded by the employer. How do you see this problem? And how should one solve it?

You should desire to remain healthy. And I think that desire, as far as we are concerned in the armed forces, was put into our heads right from the time we joined. We started getting ready for that. You have to remain healthy, and you have to be physically fit. Now that desire must be there in everyone . . . You can call it a part of discipline, or part of your learning, that you must wish to remain physically fit. If you want to stay fit, you have to first find that desire to be fit.

When did you realize that you could one day be the chief of the army staff? Did anything change in you when you recognized that one day you could be in the top job? Did it make you risk-averse? Did it make you bolder?

I don't think anyone can imagine that he may become the chief of the army one day, not till one reaches the last but one rung in the hierarchy. There are far too many factors involved: performance at each rank level, promotion examinations, selection for specialized and senior-level courses, vacancies at the next level, etc. The age factor also comes into play when you reach flag ranks. I believe it is 75 per cent hard work and 25 per cent luck when it comes to promotion to a higher level of the hierarchy.

I believe that one should 'work for the present rank and look forward to the next'. You can never shy away from the challenges that you face anytime, nor afford to be risk-averse at any level. The challenges you face in the service also become an opportunity to prove your worth. I was fortunate to have faced many challenges and opportunities throughout my career.

People at the top often say that they get lonely. Did it get lonely for you as well, considering you could not socialize freely?

I won't use the word 'lonely'. As long as you know how to interact with people, you are fine. I don't believe in a dictatorial attitude. How do you carry your team with you? You can't be a dictator in your team and then expect them to give their best. I always say that first, you must learn how to be a good team member, before you can lead a team. If you have learnt how to be a good team member, then running a team is not so difficult.

In organizations we often hear of the term man/woman management. What does man/woman management mean in a hierarchy-led organization like the army? How does one stay connected even while being in a hierarchy? This is a challenge many people face at work.

I have always given due and healthy respect to women in life. I have been married to a working woman myself and have a working daughter now living in the US. There weren't many women officers back then. But it was ensured that they got every opportunity to be groomed in the field. Cases of indiscipline, too, were dealt with strictly and exemplary punishment was awarded.

For the head of the organization, it's important to stay connected with the team. Corporate houses conduct offsites and other events for this purpose. But how did you manage that in a hierarchical organization like the army?

Right from the beginning, I learnt that it's not good enough to stay connected with your men or your subordinates;

you have to connect with them at the family level, which is unfortunately lacking in the corporate sector. They never think of the spouses or the children; they only think of the employee. And this is what I emphasize on whenever I deliver these corporate lectures. You know, someone's child may be sick, and you may not be able to ring up that person. But if your wife can ring up the child's mother, look at the kind of connection it creates. So that is something that you should do. Of course, it is easier for us in the cantonment, because it's a closed sort of atmosphere comparatively. But I think the corporate sector should learn to adopt this type of activity.

So did you make any such calls or do anything like that?

During the Kargil war, I connected myself with the troops on the ground. Every sixth day I went to the follow-up areas. And wherever I went, I would speak to my men directly. During the war, thirty-five officers had died. My wife and I both went to every officer's house, whether they were in Delhi, Chennai, Shillong or Dimapur. We went to their houses, not necessarily immediately but whenever we got the opportunity. Even today, I am in touch with those families.

I can give another example. As the army chief, you have nothing to do really when the fighting is going on. Of course, you are a part of the strategic planning and all that. But when the fighting is going on, it's not your job. You have subordinate commanders to look after that. One day,

I had gone to Drass, and I was being briefed that so and so battalion will be attacking a peak later at night. I decided to speak to the commanding officer. The officer briefing me was surprised. I am a general, and there are so many ranks in between. I spoke to him on the phone. I asked him where he was. He said, 'We are about to attack.' I just said, 'Wish you all the best. Take care.'

You have risen through the ranks, and you know exactly how to manage people. Managing people who are below you is easier. They will always take your call, they will always have time for you. But managing your superiors is a challenge, because most people get intimidated by higher designations. What tips would you have for people who feel challenged when it comes to managing their superiors?

You do your job. If you have made a mistake, you say, yes, I made a mistake. It happens. Every human being makes errors, and all of us understand it. In my case, I had to deal with politicians. Politicians never let you know what's on their mind. In that case, you have to stand by your value system and your principles. You know, you don't want to take *panga* with politicians. But you also want to, very politely, stick to your value system and the principles that you have.

Also, there is no need for anyone to unnecessarily provoke somebody just because of personal prejudices, etc. After all, a senior is a senior. Speak through your work, and stick to your principles and values.

Through your illustrious career, how did you manage the relationship with the army, the government and society? How does one manage seniors and peers in the armed forces context? What suggestions would you have on managing upwards, speaking truth to authority yet being honest in the interests of the army and the country?

Character, transparency, professionalism, moral courage, sincerity in work (no double-speaking), moderate lifestyle, no double standards. I tried to set healthy examples in all my appointments. In the kind of defence establishment that we have, I believe it is necessary to fight for the organization so that it remains fighting fit. This, too, has been a good experience. Apolitical, professional and sincere attitude has always worked. A principle I have followed is to ensure that national and organizational interests are never compromised.

Most generals end up being peacetime generals. In your tenure, you had the Kargil war. How did you mobilize the army in handling this crisis? What does it take for a peacetime general to move into war-general mode? How did your average day change?

Army maintains plans for defensive and proactive contingencies on the border. These are reviewed and updated from time to time. Mobilization of formations in peace stations for their operational tasks is an important subject. It is worked out in detail and rehearsed over and over.

The important issues in warlike situations include assessment of the situation, decision-making, the mustering and distribution of resources as per operational requirements, and ensuring synergy and orchestration of combat power at the right place. I believe that:

- Junior leaders lead the team in the field to achieve goals as laid down by senior leaders. Senior leaders manage the environment which facilitates their teams to achieve the given goals. But they must monitor the ground situation closely.
- A visit to the ground is equal to one thousand on the map.

One has to remain cool and focused, and take decisions keeping in mind the developing situation. I managed the political and military strategic environment at the services HQ in Delhi, visited senior formation headquarters to discuss the development of their operational plans and visited forward areas to monitor developing operational situations and enquire about logistical requirements and the state of the troops' morale.

It was a busy period, and required daily meetings for briefing, assessments, thinking ahead and travelling to various locations. Years of training, self-discipline and commitment came in handy.

Post retirement, all those experiences have been very useful. Soon after retirement, I was nominated as a member of the National Security Advisory Board for two terms. I helped raise ORF in New Delhi. Since 2001, I have been active as an independent director/adviser to some multinational companies. I have authored two books and written chapters and columns in books, magazines and newspapers, and have spoken of my experiences on strategic and security issues, leadership practices and motivation at universities, think tanks and public forums in India and abroad.

As head of the army, how did you envision the future of the army, and how did you direct the training and investments keeping the future in mind?

I had experience of all the major operational and logistic appointments in the army. Before taking over as COAS [chief of the army staff], I had been VCOAS [vice chief of the army staff] for one year. A month before taking over as COAS, I took a seven-day leave to consider what all improvements and changes I could bring about in the army over the next three years. Soon after taking over, I called a conference of senior commanders and discussed my intentions and work with them. After that, I let my staff issue orders, with me doing the monitoring and troubleshooting when necessary. This is the process I have followed since the time I became a Bn Cdr [battalion commander].

Every chief aspires to create a highly professional, operationally effective and cost-effective army. The geopolitical, strategic, economic and technological environment of his time matters. In my time, Pakistan and its proxy war was a greater threat. China was a long-term challenge but not a threat. The armed forces were starved economically and therefore were way behind in terms of critical holdings and modernization.

The situation today is different. China is a threat as well as a long-term challenge. Pakistan is a much weaker and lesser threat. Technology has a major impact on war-fighting capabilities. It affects our strategies, tactics and operational effectiveness. There is a need to transform—technologically, tactically, organizationally and in our human capital. Financial resources and the understanding of the functioning of the armed forces continue to be a problem. The decision-making process to face security challenges and surprises has not changed in the government.

There is much talk about the creation of the CDS, of theatre commands and so on. But the approach to achieve what was envisioned appears to me to be faulty. These are the issues that have become more relevant today.

A big event changes your life, especially if you are a part of that event. The Kargil war was one such event for you. Did it change you in some way?

When you start losing people in war, you keep thinking, 'Was it worth it?' Most of the retired generals, those who have gone through the wars, probably hate wars. They will be the ones who believe that there should be peace and that we should not go to war. I always say that one should go to war only if there is absolutely no other way out.

The loss of lives does affect you. You see wounded people and the difficulties and challenges they face. All those aspects remain alive in your mind. They just don't disappear. Every time we talk about war, you think, 'Okay, what about those aspects?' And so, all that never goes from your mind.

The other thing is that, in some way, war also makes you more broadminded. You'll start appreciating others maybe more than you do now. You know, whether it is a family or a person coming from a different background, or the kinds of challenges one is facing, regarding all those things you get a broader outlook. And maybe that is one reason why, after the war and after my retirement, I've done the kind of work I have been doing. Because you start accepting people more easily. And, you know, you make them a member of your team, or you become a member of their team. And you keep learning from them.

I can tell you that I've quite enjoyed whatever I have done after my retirement. I've never had to take orders from anybody. I made up my mind that I will not be in an organization where somebody orders me to do a particular thing. So, being independent is fine. I can ask questions. And if I don't like something, I can say, 'Thank you, I don't think I wish to continue.'

Harsha Bhogle

Harsha is the voice of Indian cricket. He studied at Osmania University and then at IIM Ahmedabad. He started in advertising and then veered to his first love, cricket, by commentating on the radio. Radio Australia invited him for a series and the rest is history, as Harsha moved into the television commentary box and made a name for himself. A Cricinfo survey voted him as the best cricket commentator. Harsha and his wife, Anita, have written a few bestsellers and they are much sought-after on the corporate speaker circuit. Harsha is on the board of IIM Udaipur. In this interview he talks about the energy one needs, about eating right and keeping fit, about his role in a field filled with ex-cricketers and the role of a captain in managing the insecurities of players.

How do you manage your time? Do you have any tips?

If there is one thing that I would like to do better, it is to manage my time better. My inspiration is my wife, Anita, because she's able to multitask so well, and to quickly move from one thing to the other and then to the other. She never wastes time. As a result, if she has eight things on her job list, she manages to get seven of them done. Whereas I am perpetually chasing my job list. People don't believe me when I say I am a little lazy. But I tend not to waste time, and I work a lot faster than other people. So, I have managed to get away, even though I have not managed my time very well.

But if I had to tell a young kid one thing, I would say manage your time very well. Don't waste time. So, one of the things I have learnt is if you're doing activity X, give it your 100 per cent. Then, when you're doing activity Y, give it your 100 per cent. When you are doing Y, don't think about X, and vice versa. If you can do that consistently, you're very good.

As a commentator you need to take a pause and not speak, especially when the action is happening. That takes a lot of discipline. Some people don't know when to speak and when to pause. How do you manage to balance this?

I am in the profession of talking, but I believe listening is by far the superior skill. You have to be able to put forward your point of view, you have to be able to articulate. But people who don't listen end up beating around the bush. If you listen well, you can be economical with your words, because then you're more focused on what you want to say. A lot of people are able to say, 'Okay, now, I'm listening.' But most of the time, when we claim to be listening, we are actually waiting for our turn to talk, and so we are actually not listening. When you are listening, you're observing people. You can find out who is insecure. You can find out who is more confident. You can find out who actually has something to say and who is just faffing. When you don't have to talk, your faculties are much more focused.

In my profession, luckily, what I say does not matter; what my colleagues say matters much more than what I say. My job is to get words out of them. So I find it easier to keep quiet. I only interrupt when they're going on for too long or we have a time issue or we have to move on to the next point.

Pausing is at the heart of speaking well. Because when you pause, it means you're breathing; it means you are gathering your thoughts; and it means you're confident.

You have a relentless day job when you are in the commentary box. You must stay focused on the game no matter what. So how do you manage your energy both in the commentary box and outside of the cricket stadium?

Broadcast and live telecast are all about energy. On television, if an anchor doesn't have energy, you lose the anchor very quickly. So, you have no option but to deliver energy, and that is why the strongest force in the world today is a hormone called adrenaline, which always kicks in. However tired I am, when the camera switches on, I am not tired, because I don't give myself that option.

You must eat well, and you must switch off. At times, sleeping well is an issue with me because my mind is whirring. You can't sleep for two, two and a half hours at least after coming back from a game. My mind is too active. But people should sleep well, because sleep is the essence of your energy. Also, in our profession, if you don't have energy, it becomes apparent straightaway.

What does a typical bad day for you look like, and how do you overcome it? On a bad day ordinary people can take leave, but you can't.

On my way to the studio, I try to stay really calm, and it's something I've learnt over the years. I didn't always have it. I find that if I am hungry or have not eaten well, then my energy levels go down, and I become crabby. When I have eaten well, I am calmer. So I try to manage food a little bit, but I also just stay calm and breathe. When I started in broadcasting, I was so tense that my producer would tell me in my ear, 'Breathe.' When you breathe, you just relax your muscles. But you cannot let a bad day get to you, because the people who are watching you don't need to know that you are having a bad day. If you lose your sense of calm, you've lost it on television.

Also, unlike the players—if a player plays one bad shot and gets out, it's the end for him—if I have done badly, I have the option of covering up for my bad performance. I often tell myself that I am not a life-saving surgeon. If I have a bad day, it's a bad day. Nobody gets hurt.

What does a day off from commentary look like?

One of my problems is that I tend to pack my day—like people pack a suitcase, and when it's full they still want to put two pairs of socks and one T-shirt in, and then they sit on the suitcase to close it. Sometimes, my days are like that. So I have to keep switching off and on. As soon as an activity ends, I switch off from it. I don't even remember it. I am learning to have a day where I clear my schedule.

How do you ensure you remain physically fit?

I take care of what I eat. I don't eat very oily stuff. It's very simple, non-spicy food. I am careful what I eat because I know I don't burn enough. But I have started walking a lot now. I love walking. I walk long distances sometimes.

The game of cricket has changed over the thirty years that you have been associated with it. How do you update yourself on the new rules, the new form of the game? And how did you develop a new vocabulary, as the nature of the audience has changed, from a bunch of die-hard cricket faithfuls who knew everything about the game to casual viewers who liked watching the IPL? How did you adapt to this change? Was there a method you used?

When you're in a T20 commentary box, you have to unlearn and forget Test cricket completely. If you look for what you found good in Test cricket, you will not find it in T20 cricket. You will find a different kind of good in T20 cricket. You have to respect change. You have to respect the fact that young kids play a certain way. You cannot say: Why is he playing like that? The game is changing.

I am not afraid of telling people I don't know [about something]. I am not afraid of going to a twenty-five-year-old kid and saying, '*Yaar, yeh mujhe samajh nahi aata* [I don't understand this].' She knows more than I do, and there is no shame in asking.

You are one of the few non-cricketer commentators. How do you manage your relationship with your co-commentators? People generally find it difficult to manage peer groups. How do you do this so well, and how have you managed to build a huge reputation for yourself?

In every team, there are some people that you get along with and some people that you don't. You just have to manage that . . . You have to be completely professional. I mean, there could be an occasion where you had a complete bust-up with somebody three minutes before going on air. Now, you are on air. But the audiences don't need to know what happened. They are saying: 'I am watching a game. I want to see you deliver your best. I want you to tell me what I need to know.' So, the moment you switch on, you are completely professional, and you completely ignore what other issues you might be having. In my case, I try very hard to make other people look good. Because that is the role of the anchor. The moment the anchor thinks, I am the star, then they are in trouble.

How have you managed your ambition over the years? Did you have any specific goals, and did you make a work plan to meet them?

One of my classmates, who is now the global marketing head of a very large lubricant oil company, would say to me: 'I have worked in this kind of company for a while. I want to now work in that kind of company for a while. Then I want a posting over here. Then I want to do this, so that I am ready for that big job.' It's like people saying, 'I want to be in sales, then maybe I want to be in the head office for a while, then maybe I want to get a little HR experience. I will then work in an MNC for a while, or I will work in one family-run company. I will be ready to be CEO after so many years.' I have never thought like that. I never said I must do a hundred games. I never said I want to be an anchor on that particular programme. Every time I went and did a programme, I said this was the best programme I could do. At the end of the programme, if it wasn't good, I would say, 'Damn, it wasn't good. Be careful next time. *Idhar problem aa sakta hai* [There could be a problem here].' So, I only stayed in the present. I think if I do the best that I can, the outcome will take care of itself and will open paths for me. Stay in the present. If in your present job you're thinking of what you need to do to get your next job, then how are you going to do your present job?

Look, this is the guy I am. I don't look like Hrithik Roshan or have a voice like Naseeruddin Shah's. There are a lot of things that I can't do. So, whatever I can do, I will make the most of it. Give everything 100 per cent. Never go unprepared and never give anything less than 100 per cent. It's not that I don't care for the future, but I know that my job requires me to be in the present. I am not saying you don't need a career plan. Have a career plan, but live in the present.

One of the important things in a company is to manage one's relationship with the organization. In your case, you have multiple organizations you work with—the ICC, the BCCI, the broadcast partner, ABC, etc. How do you manage the relationship in a proactive manner?

Not very well sometimes. There are many advantages to being who I am, but one of the hazards is that people expect me to be something. And if I am different, people don't like it. So, these tussles are always there, and you have to learn to manage those.

I learnt a lot in 2016, when I had this one year away from television. I learnt a lot because I took it badly. For about a month, I was very angry. I thought that was my only career path, but the moment that career path went away, about five other options opened. And actually, it turned out to be the best thing that ever happened to me.

In 2016, I was already fifty-five years old. But I was thrown into the world of digital and brought into contact with people my children's age. And suddenly, I found that a completely new career had just opened up for me. So, one of the things I tell people is, 'Adversity is an opportunity in different clothes.'

Always look at what your skill set is, what competitive advantage you have over somebody else. I've given up a career in advertising, a career from business school, to come into this, and I have no choice but to try and become the best. My work ethic is far better than my talent.

You run a successful company with your wife, Anita, managing corporate events, etc. Any inputs for companies/institutions on working with a successful person like yourself and how they can get the most of your time?

Keep your communication short, till you have earned the right to get more time. Be very specific about what you're asking. Don't try to be overfriendly. That's something that puts me off when young people call me. I come from a culture where people say *aap*. If somebody I don't know calls me *tu*, I switch off straightaway. Don't get overfamiliar with people.

There's one little thing about working with your spouse. A lot of my friends told me: 'At home you are together, at work you are together. I would never do that. I would just want to run away. I could never work with my wife/husband.' And I was like, 'Why?' Nobody trusts you more than your spouse. We work so well because we respect each other and trust each other.

**You have been associated with several legendary
cricket captains and their high-profile players.
Managing a team of successful cricketers could be
difficult even for a captain. Can you recall an incident
where a captain showed true leadership skills in
managing his team?**

I don't know of a single captain who was successful without
managing the insecurities of his players. Every player, at
some level or other, is insecure, even more so in corporate
life, because of their short careers. You have to understand
each of your players as a human being and as an athlete.
Some people are arrogant, some are insecure. You treat them
differently. You have to spend time as a leader to understand
the person working for you. In corporations that might be
difficult, since you have too many people working under you.
You don't have the time. In a sports team, it is easier to do.

Aarti Kelshikar

Aarti is the author of How India Works, *a book on Indian workplace culture. She is the founder of 3A Consulting and is an intercultural coach. She worked in the field of regulatory compliance in India and Singapore, and later moved to the Philippines. She is now based in Singapore and is working on her second book.*

Ninety-seven per cent of the people who start writing a book do not finish it. In this interview Aarti talks about the difficulty of writing a book, the need for discipline and energy and how lonely and difficult a task it is to write a book from start to finish. There are valuable management lessons here for every budding author.

There is a growing trend of professionals wanting to write books. You have written a book on culture in Indian organizations. What advice would you give people who are setting out to write a book?

It's easy to start writing a book, but it's not easy to finish writing it! As one works on a book, sometimes the novelty wears off and reality sets in. Which is why I feel one has to be clear as to the reason for writing. Is it because the book will help further promote your business, or because having a book to your name sounds like you have arrived? Or, to be a bit profound, is it because penning your thoughts is a meaningful extension of your purpose in life? Whatever they are, when the motivations are aligned with your values, it helps to keep you going when it gets rough or when you feel that this was not what you signed up for.

First-time writers also get bogged down thinking about who is going to publish their work or how the book's promotion will happen. My view is that once you begin writing, don't worry about how it will pan out. Writing is tedious, but it can also be fulfilling on a whole other level. Enjoy the process and go with the flow.

You have correctly pointed out that writers often drop out. About 97 per cent of people who start writing books never finish it. So, if you can tell us, from the time you ideate to the time you finish the book to the time it goes to the shelf—what are the things one should be looking at if they want to get into this domain?

It's good to chart a draft timeline, which may or may not be driven by the publisher. For example, for a non-fiction book, one could schedule a year to finish the research and writing, which would possibly get extended. As we know, it takes anywhere from six months to ten years to finish writing a book! For me, it was two years from the start to the publication of the book.

The time taken depends on factors such as how busy the author is in terms of her day job, commitments, travel, and what resources she has at her disposal to help her with the book. For authors who have a full-time job, the timelines would be different compared to what's followed by a full-time author. Either way, having a tentative timeline, with some key deliverables and dates, is a good starting point.

Also, chalking out a skeletal structure helps, especially for a non-fiction book, in terms of envisioning what the book would cover and what the focus areas should be.

Once the manuscript is finished and submitted to the publisher, it is out of the author's hands. The editing process usually takes a few months at least. And if one doesn't have a publisher, the timelines can get really unpredictable.

What kind of discipline does one need in order to write a book? Is it something that can be learnt or taught?

There is a lot of blood, sweat and tears that go into creating a book. Discipline can be a make-or-break factor. Ideally, one should keep aside a few hours daily or weekly, based on one's schedule, for writing or researching.

Yes, one can learn to be more disciplined. But in the final analysis, how driven you are determines if you can sustain momentum. You have to consciously work to make it happen. It's good to work with a timeline, but one can't be prescriptive or formulaic about this, because everybody works differently.

In my view, it helps to have some sort of accountability partners, because, in most cases, writing is a solitary process. So it's great if you have a few people whom you can share progress with and who can keep you on your toes. Otherwise, it's very easy to procrastinate.

Of course, writing cannot be just magically churned out. So many factors—including your mood, the ambience, where you write, the time of day—play a part. In terms of writing, everyone has their most productive time in a day—one should work according to that. There are great days, 'okay' days and days when you don't feel like looking at anything related to the book, which is fine because everybody needs a break. So you work on something else, and you go back to the writing when you feel like it.

The key thing is to be mindful of the timeline and, from time to time, to ensure that while you may have derailed, you aren't too far off the track. So while there is a broad structure, there is also some flexibility and fun around it. Ultimately, you need persistence and discipline, but you also need passion. It's both logic and magic.

One of the challenges people have at work has to do with data and data credibility when they quote something. So how does an author verify data and double-check it? How did you go about collecting data and analysing it?

The data from interviewees and secondary data, in terms of facts and figures, both need to be cross-checked and validated. And if one has a research assistant or somebody who has transcribed interviews, there should be enough checks and balances to make sure the data is accurately transcribed.

I make it a point to replay the entire interview and check for any omissions or mistakes in the transcript. Sometimes, even a missing word or sentence can change the meaning. This is important because, as an author, you must stand by every word written in your book.

Some people find the idea of writing books very exciting and romantic. As an author of a book—and I am told you're working on your next one—please throw light on what are the frustrations of writing a book.

It's romantic only when viewed from the outside. Just like one sees the tip of the iceberg, one sees a book with an attractive cover in a bookstore, and it seems glamorous and fairly straightforward. What isn't visible is the hard work that went into a book.

It's a slow tedious process as you build it piece by piece, chapter by chapter, cross-check and validate the information, and go through multiple iterations and rounds of self-editing to form a narrative that is coherent and insightful. You can't see the end result, and there are moments when you question the premise and the purpose! It can be frustrating, and it certainly isn't for someone who lacks patience and interest.

Often, authors tend to be their own worst critics. They keep making changes to their work or adding more data points. At some point you have to make your peace with it and say, 'This looks good enough!'

After all this, if you have a finished product that you are happy with but not the publishers, that is another hurdle to cross. But these days, one has the option to self-publish.

What personal traits and capabilities enabled you to write your first book? While working on the book, it must have been a challenge to bring to it fresh energy every day. How did you manage that? Were there days when you felt you couldn't do it?

In regard to the last part of your question, it didn't happen with the first book, but it is certainly happening with the second one! You have to make sure you have sources of positive energy to tap into. That's for everything one does, but it certainly applies to writing, as it is largely a solitary and sedentary activity. Going for long walks, meeting friends and listening to music make me feel energized and happy.

On the whole, writing a book is a labour of love, and it is incredibly fulfilling. But there are low moments that you have to be cognisant of and work around. I am mindful of my stressors and mood changes, and proactively try to steer myself to a happy, productive place.

There is no subject on which a book has not been written. If you come up with an idea to write a book, what are the ways to make it unique in order to pass the publisher's scrutiny?

An author should always check the landscape in terms of the books that are out there on the theme and introspect what he or she can do differently. Even if the theme is one that has been explored, as is often the case, what an author brings to the table is his unique perspective or viewpoint.

A case in point is the methodology for this book, and the way you have gone about weaving the narrative. By sharing your experiences and learnings, as well as incorporating those of twenty-two people from diverse backgrounds, you have managed to inject a different kind of depth, breadth and freshness to *The Art of Management*.

Who are your role models?

As in any job or field, it's always good to talk to people who have been there and done that. I recall that I spoke to a few authors and that helped me manage my expectations and prepare myself for some of the not-so-great aspects of the journey. But as far as the writing process goes, everybody's story is unique. One lives and learns, stumbles, discovers and creates!

Who inspired you to write this book?

Let me share my journey. I used to work in regulatory compliance in India and Singapore. We later moved to the Philippines, where I got into intercultural coaching, which was completely different from anything that I had done before!

For some years, I conducted customized training programmes for senior executives at multinationals. And over time, I came across books on working with Americans, the Swiss, etc. Subsequently we moved to Mumbai, where our daughter studied at an international school. We would meet expat parents who would ask questions like, 'How come Indians network so much?'; or, 'Why do Indians say "yes" and not deliver?' Things like that got me thinking: Isn't there a book on the theme of how Indians work and operate culturally, similar to the ones I had come across earlier? I couldn't find one, and that was when I decided to write one! It was perfect, given my intercultural background, professional experiences and love for writing.

Let's talk about the grand finale of every book-writing project—the launch. How was it for you? Was it easy to get an event organized? What does a book launch involve? How easy or frustrating was it for you?

I think the whole process, from start to finish, is emotional and takes a lot out of you. And the launch is special because it is your moment in the sun.

When *How India Works* came out, I thought that was the end. But I realized that while one part of the journey was over, the other, more difficult, part was just getting started. When you begin work on a book, you only think about writing it. But the truth is that in today's world, a book entails a lot of effort post-publishing. For me, this was overwhelming; it took a lot to put myself out there. I discovered that I needed a mindset and skills I hadn't signed up for!

But I learnt to deal with it. I took baby steps and reluctantly began promoting my book on social media. I spoke at various forums; I became adept at sharing the gist of my book in five minutes, and at reading an audience and thinking on my feet. I learnt the (necessary) art of managing comments and reactions on social media. And it was just amazing to hear from people I would never have otherwise heard from and to get connected with people from different parts of the world, all thanks to the book.

Looking back, it's been a fascinating ride. Getting out of one's comfort zone isn't easy, but, as they say, that's when the magic happens.

What kind of support does an author need apart from a very supportive family? Also, is it easier for a woman to be a full-time author than for men?

I think that depends on the age and the stage that a person is at. Ultimately, one does need to pay the bills, so that's a factor to consider when choosing a writing career. In the absence of financial and societal constraints, however, gender isn't as much of a factor. But the age and stage matter. One may be more ready to write in their forties, with their professional achievements under their belt and the need to do something more fulfilling.

Not many people understand or can relate to the challenges an author faces. I was lucky enough to have a few friends and family members who were incredibly supportive. They read my initial drafts, gave me feedback, heard me vent and gently nudged me along. Most importantly, they believed in me.

And the last question I have is about COVID? Did it in any way help you as a writer when you began writing your second book?

I began my research for my second book just as the pandemic started. I had this whole plan of travelling to a few countries to meet and speak with people as research for my book. Obviously, that didn't happen, so I was disappointed to begin with. But then I realized that it was actually easier to get dates and times for meetings as people weren't travelling and were working from home. So it became easier and more efficient.

It is amazing to see how, in the past two years, we have all navigated the various constraints of connecting and operating in a virtual world without borders and boundaries.

Shereen Bhan

*Shereen is easily the most recognizable of Indian TV journalists.
We have all seen her covering the World Economic Forum, Davos,
beat and she was ahead of her time when she started and anchored*
Young Turks, *a programme celebrating entrepreneurship.*

*In this interview she talks of her choices, about moving into
anchoring, picking her words and phrases and maintaining the
confidentiality of her sources. She also talks about the challenges
of being a woman leader and how she navigates them.*

**You are one of India's most recognized journalists. Is
this success more an outcome of your work and not so
much of your ambitions and goals?**

My role as an anchor at CNBC-TV18 was something that
happened really by accident. I hadn't thought of it when I
started my career as a producer in UTV. I was doing political
journalism, and I was behind the camera, producing shows.
When the HR team at CNBC reached out to me, it was for

an upcoming political news channel. The interview went well. I was told that it was going to take a couple of months. Within a few hours, I got a call from the HR person again, saying, 'Can you come back tomorrow? Raghav [Bahl] wants to meet you.' I met Raghav, and he said, 'Have you thought of anchoring?' And I said, no, it's never been an aspiration. He asked me to do an audition. I was not prepared, but I did it. After I finished, he asked, 'Can you join tomorrow?'

So that was really how this started. I never started my career as an anchor, though I've always been very clear about the fact that I wanted to get involved with all aspects of broadcast journalism—whether it's producing my own shows, writing my own scripts, editing, going on shoots, handling logistics, coordination. I've done everything on virtually every show that I've ever worked on. So when I started at CNBC, I was producing the morning primetime show, which is still the number one stock market show in India. I was working on that as a producer, and I was anchoring shows like *Business Lunch*. I wanted to work on all aspects of broadcast journalism, and this helped me understand how things work end to end and develop myself more holistically as a professional.

The other thing is that I've never focused on having a particular goal. I always wanted to do stuff that was not being done, to do things differently. I wanted to create my own niche, my own space. There were people I looked up to, such as Prannoy Roy, for his presence, his poise. He had a distinct niche. I didn't want to become just another anchor in an assembly line of anchors. So I worked on developing skills that would help me hold my own. I developed an attitude of being open to trying new things, learning from my peers but not forcing myself into a particular template.

I'll give you another example. When CNBC-TV18 decided to move headquarters from Delhi to Bombay in 2006, I was anchoring a lot of the market shows. I said to Raghav: 'I don't want to move to Bombay because I've always been associated with policy and political journalism, and when I moved to CNBC I had managed to create space for political talk shows. Plus, Delhi's been home for me.' He told me very clearly: 'Look, if you're going to stay on here, then all the market shows are going to go from you, and you are going to lose a lot in terms of visibility.'

It wasn't an easy decision to make. But I decided to take the risk. Suddenly I was off air and people were noticing my absence. It was hard for me. But it pushed me to create new shows. I moved to doing shows like *India Business Hour* and moved from the morning team to the team focused on corporate and policy news.

I could have become completely irrelevant to the organization if I had just said, 'Okay, this [moving to Bombay] is the worst thing that's happened to me.' But I decided to use that as an opportunity for me to explore things that interested me, and to make myself relevant again to the organization in a different way and create something that the organization would also benefit from.

I've always been more mindful of collective success, not so much personal. I developed deep relationships with people across teams, and this really helped me later, when I became the managing editor. The ability to take the organization along, the ability to get different groups of people to work together, the ability to break down silos, I believe, became possible because I had built a rapport with people over the years.

We live in a social world where individuals are brands. You are a brand in your own right. What do you think of Shereen the social brand vs Shereen the media personality? How do you manage your personal brand?

One of the things that I've been very mindful of is that I've never believed in this business of 'I am bigger than the brand' or 'I am the star', because I realize how ephemeral it all is. I think a lot of people in our business tend to get a little carried away with the personal brand.

CNBC, as a brand, stands for providing actionable, verifiable information in real time that is of use to people in their daily lives. My own brand stands for pretty similar things. I am really an extension of CNBC. I am not one of those people who have an opinion on everything. I will talk about things that I understand. I will talk about or voice my opinions about things that I am interested in or that I actually know enough about to make an informed comment on. When I am working on a show, if I am doing an interview, I go in there assuming that it is probably the last show I am going to do. So I have to give it my best. And that is a key attribute of my brand promise—giving people meaningful information in 30–60 minutes. I don't take the time that viewers spend on us for granted. I believe that if someone is watching my show, then she/he must get some value from investing that time on me. So, CNBC-TV18 and my brand are aligned, and I don't think it can be any other way.

It is absolutely crucial to stay healthy and radiant when you are on TV. How do you manage to look so cool, calm and fresh day in and day out? What health practices do you follow? I have never seen you hassled on air. How do you do that?

I believe that if somebody is going to be spending thirty minutes or an hour of their time watching you, they need to feel a sense of connection, have confidence in the person they are tuning into day after day. I have very consciously stayed away from what has now become popular, this 'noise TV' journalism, because I can't watch it myself. I've been very clear about my on-air persona as well. I would like to be seen as someone who is clear, fair, accurate and delivers the news with integrity. I guess most people relate to that. And people acknowledge that I can ask tough questions, but I don't need to be rude or offensive or raise my voice to make an impact . . .

There's no particular health regimen I follow. I do yoga, on and off. And I walk as much as possible. I do most of my calls walking.

A voice which is pleasing to the ear is one of the most important assets in your profession. How do you manage to keep your voice cheerful, youthful and distinct?

I am mindful of the way I speak. There are times when I see I am speaking too fast. Because in your head you feel like, okay, you've got only ten minutes left for the show, but you're trying to pack in all the information that you have, and so you tend to speed things up. I think what's important is the ability to not just listen to yourself but also to develop the art of listening to others. People go into an interview with ten questions and try to be done with it. I think if you stay so focused on what is on paper and stop listening to what is actually happening in the conversation, you may lose out on elevating the conversation beyond the obvious. Some of my best interviews have actually been a result of picking up on what the person told me during the course of the conversation, which was probably not on the list of twenty questions that I went in there with.

One of the challenges for senior management has to do with language—repetition of pet phrases, catch phrases, etc. How have you worked on your vocabulary over the years? Do you have any deliberate system to widen your vocabulary?

As a channel we aim to simplify the language. And we have been successful to some extent but I don't think nearly as successful as we ought to be. This is something someone told me, many years ago: if you're explaining an idea, or your mission or vision or company statement, you should be able to do it in a manner that even my grandmother could understand! I think very often in our business, people have this know-it-all attitude, and that sort of stymies your learning and your development. I am always open to learning, whether it's from a kid who has just joined or from a peer.

You are an ace presenter, and you also are responsible for the P&L of the business channel. How do you manage to straddle both these roles?

I am not directly responsible for the P&L. But I do work with the CEO as well as the sales and marketing teams on developing new revenue streams and business ideas that have been taken to market. I have been focused on making CNBC-TV18 much more than just a TV channel. Today, we have a 360-degree presence, and that is something I have worked on refining over the past few years.

Did you ever think that you were competing with men for anything? Or perhaps this didn't figure in any way in your thinking. If it did, how did you handle this issue?

I didn't feel like I was competing with men. But when I took on a leadership role, I did feel that my being a woman had its constraints. There was a camaraderie the men shared, and an access that they enjoyed, which did not naturally extend to me. And so, it was harder to break into the decision-making roles. While I was responsible for execution, I felt I wasn't as closely involved in the decision-making. We are an inherently patriarchal society. If I am doing an event, very often I am the only woman on the panel, and I have often noticed that at the time of introductions, comments would be made about how I look! While it is well-meaning and meant as a compliment, it is not relevant to the reason I was invited for! Now, when somebody makes a comment like that, or a flippant comment like comparing the stock markets to the temperament of a woman, etc., which is something I have heard very often over the years, I call them out and tell them that their comment was inappropriate.

Considering all these challenges, you still have managed to build a very good social network. How have you managed to develop your network over the years?

I think it really boils down to the experience that people have when they engage with you. If I do an interview with someone, and the interviewee walks away from that interview saying, 'Hey, this was one of the best conversations I've had', they treat you with respect, and remember that experience.

I remember we did this big event at IIT Delhi. This was the first time that the then newly appointed CEO of Uber, Dara Khosrowshahi, was visiting India. I had worked on this for a few days. I read up everything there was to read about him. And so, I was well prepared. I think he was surprised by the information and particularly the anecdotes that I brought up in our conversation, because he could see the effort I had made to understand his journey. As he was leaving, he told me it was one of the most engaging conversations he'd had.

Confidentiality is a key success factor when you are getting information from various sources. How do you manage to get people to tell you things in confidence? This is a challenge for most corporate executives.

I think that the fundamental premise of any relationship and, more importantly, for any source–journalist or interviewer–

interviewee relationship is trust. Someone is telling you something in confidence, and they expect you to respect that. It's absolutely imperative that you don't breach that trust, unless and until the information shared is something of significant public importance. The tendency to brag about your connections or access to somebody is very off-putting. I don't appreciate name-dropping.

How up to date are you with technology personally?

Not much. I was forced to get on WhatsApp because of all these groups that have now been created. But I am a very reluctant social media person or WhatsApp person. Even on Twitter, I focus on the content we create or information that is relevant to our audience. I voice my opinion on issues that I can contribute to. I am not a very active social media person. I am not a very tech-savvy person. I have a passive social media relationship.

N.S. Rajan

Rajan is an HR master. He did a PhD in leadership from IIT Delhi and did his MBA at XLRI. He started the HR practice in EY and went on to lead it. He then moved to the Tata Group as member, GEC. After the Tata stint, he moved to IDFC. There is little that Rajan does not know about HR and its application across industries. He is on the board of XLRI.

Rajan has published a number of books and is a popular speaker in management circles. In this interview he talks about discipline, good habits, the strength of listening, managing emotions, managing peers at work and why he thinks the matrix organization is tough to work in.

What are some of the good executive habits and bad executive habits that you have observed over the years in executives?

Our habits, metaphorically, are like the food we eat—what is good for us may taste bad, and what tastes bad may actually be good for us.

One habit, which one must learn to avoid, when we lead people, is to rebuke in public and reward in private. The ideal way to do it is the other way around. When we pull up someone with other people around, the recipient, instead of understanding what needs to be corrected, is more concerned with what others may think of him.

When we assume a senior position, some abuse their power and often take undue liberties with those below them in the hierarchy. In my mind, true power is in having it and never having to use it; we need to use the power vested in us to empower and help, rather than command and control. Lack of such prudence can only hurt us in the long run.

Another common habit that we must learn to eschew is our tendency to procrastinate. Those who constantly postpone things will find every tomorrow an extra-busy day. It leads to a vicious cycle where decision-making becomes impossible. The problem at hand often gets worse and those around are disempowered. Exceptions are rare, and only a gifted few can, perhaps, escape the problem at hand by deliberately postponing a decision and allowing the problem to become insignificant. For lesser mortals, it is advisable to get things done on time.

Another common folly is the habit of wanting to do everything yourself and, perhaps, believing that you are the best person to do it. When one transitions from being an individual contributor to being a manager, the key competence involves getting things done by others. This becomes even more critical as we take on higher roles. Those who believe that they themselves do it best will stop others from learning and doing what they actually can. Moreover, you regress rather than progress in delivering well in your designated role. A CEO, for example, may not know every single function as well as others do and yet is able to achieve the necessary outcomes by leading rather than micromanaging. A team leader need not necessarily know how to cook, but one surely needs to know what's cooking.

What characteristics are important to manage oneself at work?

One of the most important things for me is investing time in listening to people. Your ability to invest time in listening to people is a very important part of managing yourself and in your growth as a leader.

Another critical need is your openness to the feedback that you receive. In formal environments, we have a system of feedback where the boss is the one who is expected to give it. But feedback from younger people, peers and stakeholders is vital for personal growth. When I see someone who is open to feedback and also works on it, I see a leader in the making.

Sensitivity to others' needs, and not just one's own, is also vital in managing oneself. You can't be a good leader of people if you don't understand their needs, unravel their fears and anticipate their hopes. This requires us to be compassionate at work, even while being tough on work-related expectations.

What advice do you have for people on managing emotion at the workplace?

Emotions are a part of us. So, I feel sad, I feel happy, I feel angry, I feel hatred, and all of them play a role in making us who we are. I also believe that there is nothing like a negative emotion, as every emotion has its place, for reasons known or unknown. Let me take anger, for example. If I express anger, it means I want to control others. At the same time, when I am angry, it also means I am not in control of myself. If that's the case, what authority do I have to try to control you? That's why it's best to keep anger where it emanates: your own mind. It's also important to recognize that when I get angry, I miss the issue and focus on the person. The only time anger is useful and helpful is when you 'show' you're angry but actually you are not, because then you're in total control of yourself.

The way to manage emotions is to ensure that a flaw doesn't turn into a fatal flaw, which will actually eclipse the other virtues you may possess. When we learn to manage our emotions, and learn not to cross the line, that is where our emotional quotient is best reflected. The most effective way to use our emotions, seemingly good or bad, is to recognize them and practise moderation.

How does one manage peers in an organization? Any tips you can offer based on your observations?

Peers have always been a troublesome zone, and I must confess that it is easier to work with those who are much younger or much older than you. When people are at the same level, the reason for a disconnect may be that they are competing with each other, insecure about each other and perhaps want greater attention and opportunities, in relative terms. Managing peers requires alignment to common goals, respect for each other and the willingness to co-create.

How do you see ambition at the Indian workplace? Do we like people who are ambitious? Or do we like people who put their head down and just work?

I think human progress has really been a function of two things: ambition and discontentment. Ambition because you wish to progress, and therefore you want to conquer more. Discontentment is when you're unhappy with the current state of things. And that pushes you to find a better way to handle what happens around you or what needs to be accomplished. There is both ambition and the lack of it, in all workplaces. I have always found it easier to handle those with ambition than those who are content being mediocre.

Each enterprise, like an individual, has a personality and a character. So a lot depends on the nature of the organization, and you cannot assume a generic principle that Indian workplaces don't value ambition. If that were the case, we wouldn't have had so many entrepreneurial success stories. You can't be an entrepreneur if you lack ambition.

There are a lot of concerns about bosses. How does one get the most out of a good boss, and what are strategies for handling a bad (insecure/incompetent) boss?

I have been lucky to have many great bosses who have contributed to my success and growth. When you report to a good leader, the need to manage your boss is minimal, as all you need to focus on is giving your best. Managing poor bosses is another thing altogether. It is easier to know a poor boss than to define one. For instance, if one is a non-performer, a demanding leader may feel like a bad leader. For all you know, you yourself may be a bad employee rather than having a bad boss.

Surviving them is tougher than managing them, particularly if they are incompetent and insecure. You may not be in a position to alleviate the underlying root of the problem, but there are things you can do to ensure you don't fuel the fire.

Don't say things about having a bad boss to everyone around. Never bypass and skip levels, unless that is the last resort. Never show off, if you know more than your boss. Never forget to inform your boss if his boss speaks to you directly. Never dissent in public and keep your conflicts between you and your boss. Never fail to give credit where it is due. Try to use friends outside of the workspace to share your woes—they might help you handle it better, as they can be objective.

If all of this fails, do what the Japanese supposedly do. Employees are provided with a life-sized doll that resembles the boss, or you could assume it to be so, and beat the hell out of it. That should help release all your anger and help you accept him with greater calm and composure when you deal with him in person. You have found a way to express your angst!

Sometimes, despite doing your best, there are things beyond your control that don't help with your progress. How does one deal with such situations?

Adversity is a part of life. I have always believed that every problem has a solution, and if it doesn't have any, you are dealing with a fact, not a problem. You can't change facts, but you can surely find ways to recognize and accept them. The best way to thrive and survive is to continue doing your best and wait for the tide to turn.

Take a look at what happened to all of us in COVID times. Despite all your effort at work, there are things beyond your control and the only way out is to adopt the new way of life and also get ready to make a comeback when things settle down. In every walk of life, be it work or otherwise, you must find a way to do all you can and be the best you can. Even the mighty ocean experiences low tides.

Who are good team leaders? What do good team leaders do better than average team leaders?

Let me share one aspect that has been of significance. Good leaders understand the strength and weakness of each of the team members and find a way of helping them individually excel and yet towards a common direction. A good leader also ensures that one is able to complement a team member's capabilities with one's own. This involves encouraging team members to deliver on their strengths and fill in for their weaknesses.

How does one handle team members who place their interests ahead of the team's?

Cooperation, collaboration and an environment that rewards teaming are essential to building a culture that enables mutual growth. Enabling meritocracy at the workplace further establishes an objective platform. It is but natural that anyone's first concern would be one's own growth and progress. As leaders, we need to be fair, remain objective and recognize those who team well. On the one hand, it is important to mine individual brilliance, but it's equally essential to harness collective capability. When we deal with someone who is selfish and less interested in others, it is the role of the leader to reinforce the value of going beyond oneself.

What advice would you have for working in a matrix?

If you ask me, the matrix system never really works. It's like having more in-laws than you need. A multiplicity of bosses can be difficult for employees to manage, as it lessens clarity on the way forward and leads to an absence of final accountability. A common matrix is to have dual reporting to a sales head and a product head. It would, perhaps, work only in a few organizations, where the two bosses are so completely aligned with each other that their goals are one. That's rather rare.

What should be an employee's relationship with an organization?

Any fulfilling relationship requires both parties to invest in it. In organizations, it should be one of a shared purpose and vision, with an alignment of goals and a mutual commitment to each other. A relationship is built and reinforced when there is trust.

How do you see workplace loyalty today and in the future?

You know, this word 'loyalty' has multiple connotations. Expecting loyalty from an employee is a fallacy, and to treat longevity as evidence of loyalty is an even bigger fallacy. In current times, when loyalty is scarce and longevity is unlikely, our focus needs to be on making every day of an employee special. One must be loyal to the work on hand, every single day—to be productive, as an individual and for the enterprise. In days of yore, promoters and CEOs often expected personal loyalty, rather than professional loyalty. You can no longer treat an employee as a subject and subject them to such expectations. Build and invest in professionals, and enable a deeper commitment to work, rather than insisting on loyalty. We must also recognize that just as an enterprise expects to grow, so the individual employee has aspirations to blossom. If we cannot provide them avenues to ensure mutual growth, don't expect them to be around. Birds with wings will fly away if you don't care to nurture them.

What advice would you have for the average employee on learning to stay relevant?

I believe that it is vital to focus on what I refer to as the 'T' model of learning. That is to ensure you learn to go deep in a vertical of choice but also to keep building knowledge of other fields as a horizontal, to the extent you can. Unless you're a Da Vinci, you may not be able to master multiple domains with equal expertise. It is important, though, to recognize that our chosen function has many adjacencies and interdependencies, which can help us deliver better.

As regards a particular field you have embraced, the real differentiation is in being able to go as deep as you can and be at the cutting edge of knowledge in that area. Be the expert who can be granular in approach and is constantly expanding the boundaries of the domain that is your vocation. Learn to deliver well on what is required to be accomplished today; anticipate and be ready to seize tomorrow as it unfolds.

What skills are needed for a future world?

An open-ended question, indeed, and I may not have a comprehensive answer to this. Some of the competencies that come to mind are:

- Embracing diversity and inclusion, not tokenism.
- Enabling a digital way of life, not just technology.
- Enhancing crowd-sourcing and co-creation, not relying on individuals alone.
- Effective crisis management, not reactive but proactive.

Vikas Khanna

Vikas is an inspiration. He is regarded as one of the best chefs in the world, a Michelin-starred chef. Vikas has a fascination for food ingredients and it is a learning to listen to him speak of the various ingredients, their history, etc. He has published a number of books, and each one is pictorially brilliant—every picture painstakingly taken by Vikas himself.

Vikas did a lot of selfless work during COVID, arranging food for many people across the country. In this interview he talks about the value of hard work, innovation in food, dreaming big and making an impact.

How have you managed this journey from Punjab to New York, and what challenges did you face on it?

I realized very early on that you have to choose your battles. I have to be laser-focused, because of the kind of benchmarks that I set for myself. Every time I do something, I am setting a benchmark. But while focus is great, being unfocused is just as important. Sometimes I need to unfocus on a few things. Because we all have twenty-four hours. So, almost everyone gets similar opportunities, but somehow most people don't focus on the right priorities.

Sometimes that happens with me as well, where you feel that you've wasted your time. While managing yourself, the most important part is time. Another thing that I figured out very early on was that talent means nothing without hustling.

I live in New York City, which is the most talented city on the planet. But so many failed people are so talented. I have so many chefs around me who are more talented than me. But they somehow don't understand time management. We are taught that managing our time is the only currency we have.

How do you look at your career and your life today?

I have worked with a lot of good chefs. But Michelin-starred chefs are so much better at management and delegation, disciplined in terms of innovation, self-discipline and being focused. They focus just on one thing on the plate and the discipline of the kitchen. And while we have other chefs whom I have worked with, they were so focused on politics. They were so focused on *kisne kya bola, kaun upar ja raha hai, kaunsa restaurant fail ho raha hai* [who said what, who is rising, which restaurant is failing]. And that was what I learnt when I was working with a lot of chefs who were substandard. Nepotism can't win you a Michelin star. The only way humans are quantified in terms of their cooking skills is through a Michelin star, and I won it in the world's most competitive city, and won it six consecutive times. I hope more Indian chefs go beyond this and set new benchmarks. But they have to move away from politics.

One of the reasons people don't think I am very successful in the restaurant industry is that I don't have fast-food restaurants or substandard restaurants around the world. I don't measure myself on those benchmarks. There are thousands of chefs. Many of them are just focused on Instagram views and not on training. We just hired a French chef, whom I paid for to come to New York just so that I could learn one dish from him. Everybody thinks this is crazy—you can't be spending $10,000 just to learn that one dish. And I said that the chef deserves it, and that I am going to use my time to be inspired and make more dishes from that one dish. People think that the learning process is over.

You are one of the leading lights in your craft. What does it take to be globally acclaimed? What does it take to stay at the top of your profession for so many years?

Honestly, success is very blinding. It's an illusion. You attract friends who are actually not your friends; you attract investors who are not the right people to support you. You attract a very different group of people. The only thing that keeps me grounded is speaking to my mom two times a day. I know a lot of people think this is not a part of management, but it works for me. I come under a lot of scrutiny because I am an Indian chef. But people don't understand how much hard work I put into everything I take up. I am not doing buffet restaurants. We aspire to be the Mercedes or the Lamborghini of Indian food.

Speaking to my mom helps me stay motivated, because she is not bothered about what's happening in the restaurant industry or to chefs. It's good for your mental health to stay connected with some people who are actually there for you. I also believe that sanity is important, health is important. I am one of the few Michelin-starred chefs who've come out and spoken about mental health.

A lot of people who climb the ladder, the first thing they do is disconnect from those who are there for them. Because you want everybody to worship you and notice your crown. But my mom doesn't do that and has been the force that has kept me grounded through my entire career, for almost thirty-five years.

You are one of the few Indians to have won a Michelin star. What does it take personally to make it to the Michelin list?

When I was working in France, in 2008, a chef told me, 'You know, the reason we don't hire Indian chefs in top positions is because they are absolutely based on copy-paste. They do exactly the same menus, and that's why Michelin never pays attention to you.' He was right. We have exactly the same menus, which I too had been selling in New York for so long. That is why we don't get attention. For appetizers, you have samosa, kachori, chaat, chicken tikka, seekh kebab, and so on and so forth.

If everybody's doing exactly the same thing, there is nothing that will bring you to the attention of the *New York Times* or the *Michelin Guide*. Michelin is not paying attention to you because you are not making an effort. Michelin is looking for something which is innovative. So, innovation is key. If people have to grow in their respective fields, they need to innovate. But innovation also has a dark side to it. It alienates you from the native people. If you come to my restaurant and you don't see any familiar dishes, that can result in a disconnect. Risk-taking is very dangerous, because you know that if you introduce a new dish on the menu and it doesn't sell, the owner and investors will come after you and ask you to sell something 'regular' which people would want to buy. You require effort, and money, to innovate.

What is your learning style? How do you learn, and how do you keep abreast of developments in your business?

Our developments are mostly happening in Europe. France became the leader of innovation in cooking. And then, of course, the Japanese, the British and the Americans took it to the next level. Americans also incorporate a lot of business models with artistic models. I like to incorporate the business part of it, because I want the restaurants to be full. And I can't have a niche restaurant with only ten patrons. So I figured out that learning was very important. But one has to be very careful while learning. You can't just look at a French Michelin-starred restaurant and say, 'Let's copy the menu.' That won't take you to the next level. Overlearning is also a big problem. Chefs who know too much, they don't want to go back to the basics and understand that the market might not want something. Learning has to be compatible with the market's purchasing power.

What is the role of time in your craft, and how did you learn to manage/master time?

My biggest challenge is time zones. We have a restaurant in Dubai. We have one coming up in Hong Kong, which is in an opposite time zone. We work in India for most of our creative projects, and we are otherwise based in Eastern Standard Time. I ran the entire Feed India initiative based on the Indian time zone. So, imagine: you're feeding close to 65 million people, and everything is based on an opposite time zone for you.

Time management means I have to be alert twenty-four hours, and that takes a toll. But I do feel that it is also a great opportunity for a chef, for any artist, to work in many time zones. This also shows that you're reaching out to a much bigger global market . . . The reason we manage time so well is that we are choosing the right projects. I cannot choose projects based on money. When you get to a level, you are surprised at how many opportunities come to you based on just money transactions. But I don't want to be an ATM. I want to have a soul.

What is the role of technology in your craft, and how have you come to grips with it?

Right now, most of our work is running on technology. Because of COVID, we can't travel everywhere. So much of the work is actually happening on Zoom calls, where I cook simultaneously with my team. I cook a dish here at my house, and they are cooking the same dish, and you're documenting the recipes. It's all technology. Technology is amazing right now. Managing the restaurant, staff, payrolls, the scheduling—technology is the only thing actually helping us to be more efficient, especially when you're going global.

You are known for innovation in food. How do you think of innovation, and how do you know an innovation has worked? How do you go about innovating?

So many times we fail. One benefit is that we have a multicultural team.

While innovating we sometimes get too carried away and think, 'Oh my god, this is just not making any sense.'

Now, if you're doing a fish sauce, you need to have learnt a new technique. And you should be able to show off and flaunt the quality of the meats or seafood or vegetables you use. If everything is drenched in that same soupy-looking sauce, you won't even be able to assess the quality of the meat and ingredients that were used.

But in India, what happens is that we put everything in a stew. In France, it's unacceptable. If you have a piece of fish, you need to season it and cook it fresh. Then you have to put a warm fresh sauce under it and then garnish it. Imagine the effort that goes into serving the same dish. The effort which it takes to innovate a dish is insane.

I get trolled every time I put a new dish on social media. People are like, 'What's the point, chef? *Roti toh roti hoti hai* [a chapati is a chapati].' I agree. But clothes, too, are just clothes. So then why do you wear Prada? Why do you save money to buy a Mercedes? If we think like that, we will never have aspirational value to our lives.

How do you spot innovations?

I don't sleep on Saturday nights, because that's when I write. So Sunday is when I innovate. On some days the innovation fails; on some days you know you're not up to it; and on some days it works like magic. Also, now the world has changed. Social media has given us a lot of ways to watch things at a much faster speed, and it's a big source of inspiration.

One of the things every business does is to scale up a successful formula. In your field, how big can a successful idea become?

My biggest restaurant, which I put so much energy into for years and years, totally failed. I used to have a restaurant in the heart of Times Square, and I said it was going to work.

Sometimes things work for you, and it is like, boom!—and the rocket takes off, and it's in space. It doesn't even need any fuel. The only formula I have is: don't stop hustling. Even when something works, you still can't stop hustling, because the world is changing around you.

I have figured out that the food industry is so massive that you need to find your own stop. Expanding to big cities, which we have the capacity of doing, would drive me insane. Not that I am scared of risks. Post COVID, we're going to look for relief in food. We saw people taking shelter in kitchens. I feel that we have now realized the healing power of our kitchens. There's no limit to how much we can go forward in our cooking right now. Because food is something which is going to give us a whole different high. The food industry has infinite capacity.

You are always contributing back to society, you did a lot of work for Covid, how do you pick which cause to choose and why? How do you match the Vikas Khanna brand with the cause?

You know the initial thing was a disaster because we were thinking that we need to feed people. We saw lines of people waiting for food and how mismanaged it looked. So, my branding manager said, 'You know what this is, this might be the one of the biggest campaigns in the world, the way you are envisioning, but it has to be a Michelin-star standard campaign.' We just served khichdi without any daal, because the daal was going bad due to the heat. Even that was done with so much dignity. I had issues when the team in India didn't have the same sensibility the way we wanted. I said anything we put out is reflecting on how my brain works. The discipline, production or distribution was par excellence.

Are you a perfectionist?

No, a work-in-progress, but with dignity. It's very easy to be a clone. Most of the Indian industry is inspired by Sanjeev Kapoor. And so am I. He is the pioneer and will continue to inspire generations. But I always like to add my own touch, my innovation signature to everything I do. For me, it's very important to be original. To make it in the US, you have to be original. Though great teachers show you the path, you will have to write your own story.

I am sure you had disappointments on your journey. How does a high achiever like you handle disappointments?

I'm amazing at dealing with failures. The moment I feel I can't save it, it is gone. Next morning, I will focus on something completely different. Even relationships, even in contracts . . . if something fails, I move on to the next project. You have to disconnect yourself, and you have to jump on to something more challenging, because failure or disappointment or betrayal gives you such amazing energy. It's like a fuel, which you can't have in success. There is no time to sit and cry.

How do you manage social media? Do you see it as a tool that helps you, or is it something you need to guard against?

I have been very organic on social media. And I've always been very accepting of others. But if fire can cook your food, it can also burn your house down. So you need to tame that fire. The guy who runs my account posts some generic comments, but we try to avoid too much engagement. I use it very sensibly and make sure that I don't overdo it.

Managing Yourself: Points for Reflection

1. The key to managing yourself is D E F: Discipline, Energy and Focus.

2. The world is changing quickly and no degree from the past will see you through. Concepts have shorter shelf life and many are just fads. Reskill every year, you will need it. Giving back as a teacher in every discipline is important to develop the craft.

3. Being the absolute best in your chosen field is a worthwhile ambition to have. Ambition fuels progress and sets new benchmarks; personal ambition on its own is good only in a few cases.

4. Peers, followed by bosses, will challenge you the most in life. Managing your peer group in any sphere is not easy. Seeking common ground with peers, holding your ground when needed for the institution and your team helps.

5. Managing time will give you a head start in life and keep you there. Being late at work is the top reason for dismissal in America! Time will be monetized this decade as the support system to deliver everything on time will develop—groceries, advise, medicines, construction.

Section II

Managing Your Team

All of us want to be regarded well by people who work for us. In that quest, some of us try to become popular, some of us try to become strict, and some of us try to be ourselves.

In every sphere, we start as individual contributors before we get assigned to lead a team. Being a good individual contributor and excelling at it catches the eyes and ears of our superiors, and then they assign us to managing a team.

A team by definition is a bunch of diverse people and diverse talents. A good leader will try and harness the diversity in the team as opposed to making them work in his/her prescribed way.

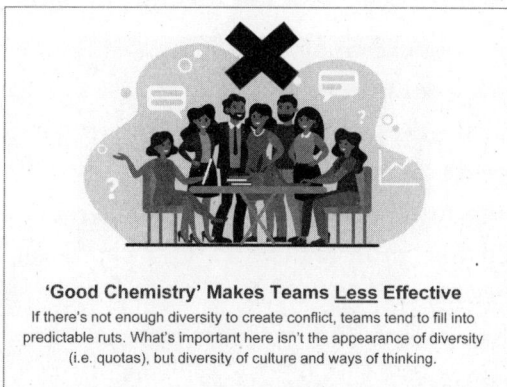

'Good Chemistry' Makes Teams <u>Less</u> Effective

If there's not enough diversity to create conflict, teams tend to fill into predictable ruts. What's important here isn't the appearance of diversity (i.e. quotas), but diversity of culture and ways of thinking.

Image source: https://www.freepik.com/
Source: https://www.inc.com/geoffrey-james/10-surprising-scientific-facts-about-teams.html

A common mistake all managers make when they lead a team is to prescribe what they want the team to do. This could be done through the formats managers give their team, the structure of thinking they provide the team with, or by setting the ground rules to be followed by the team or giving instructions on how the work should be done. I think every team leader should provide an organizational framework of how the team is to work as opposed to a personal framework.

If you want to be a good team leader, think about the following:

> Being fair
> Being consistent
> Being a coach without imposing your personality
> Handling the prima donnas and the weight-carriers in a team

Being Fair

Fairness is about exercising good judgement and honesty in dealing with team members. It is about the display of basic respect and dignity at the workplace, in terms of language used and credit given.

A workplace or team cannot be too sterile; if it is too sterile, then you get insipid work. So, a good team will not try and make everything a rule or a process. A good team and its leader manage the inconsistencies and tensions in a harmonious way.

Fairness is an innate value. There is no training course to teach fairness. Being fair means you have to deal with much baggage and context. At work, it is difficult to be fair when you have worked with some people longer than others and when you have done multiple stints with some people. There is a natural tendency to listen to and promote people you know better. It's important to guard against this, so that everyone in your team, young or old, tenured or fresher, feels they have a chance.

If we look at sports, every captain and every manager picks the team they believe can win on that day, in those conditions. They are taking a calculated gamble. When it turns out well, they are seen as great strategists; when it fails, they are seen as duds.

Being fair also means calling a spade a spade and enforcing company policy when someone steps out of line. Turning a blind eye is not fairness—it is actually unfair on people who are doing the right thing. I have had to call out people in my teams who would selectively pick up the team agenda and let others do more of the work. For example, some people will want to work on projects which have a presentation potential to the CEO and avoid projects which do not have exposure to the senior management. In every instance I have called out the inconsistencies to ensure that the team is in a better place.

Fairness also means that you need to rethink some archaic rules that don't apply any longer. Today's employee is a volunteer. Volunteers have a choice. Much like we volunteer for causes we believe in, employees can choose companies based on what the company stands for. In the future, the way we treat employees who work from home will determine the strength of fairness in a team or organization. For example, in a COVID situation, do you allow employees to choose a safer but more expensive hotel that is above their limit, or do you stick to rules and ask them to stay within their limits? I have always asked employees to do what's right from the health point of view. Will you provide employees with a car service as opposed to asking them to use a ride-sharing app? These test the limits of fairness and the contradiction between rules and context.

Innate Fairness at Work

Opportunity Fairness

Signs of Innate Fairness at Work

Open Feedback

Process and Communication

Source: https://ifs.org.uk/inequality/wp-content/uploads/2020/11/Fairnessacross-the-world-Preferences-and-beliefs.pdf

Another instance when you can rethink the rules is when women return to work after maternity leave. I don't think we are doing them a favour by giving them a role or a job. I think the team leader must go out of the way to ensure that some rules are rewritten so her joining back is smoother.

The issue of fairness comes up most starkly when people see the promotion list in an organization. If they feel that the list is full of yes men/women, then there will be no talk of fairness in the company. If the list is largely meritorious, then people will believe that fairness exists in an organization. I always wanted the management team to pitch in on every promotion and thus get broader consensus on who we promote. Promotions decided by the CEO alone, or by the CEO and the CHRO, could be biased and may not take the full picture into account.

Fairness is about whether junior people in the company are getting their due for the work they have done. If in an organization the seniors are taking all the credit and the juniors are feeling left out and frustrated, then there is no fairness. A good leader needs to judge people's contribution at work fairly.

Fairness is whether you are compensated adequately for your talent and performance. I once had a manager who thought his performance was great but the performance of his subordinates was bad. I challenged him to explain that to me, and in the end I had to pull up the ratings of the subordinates and pull down the self-rating of this manager. You have to judge who are the people who will line up at the head of the line for credit and who are at the back of the line but deserve to be at the front. When I was at PepsiCo, I remember that a lot of women felt they were not being paid a fair salary. When I got the analysis done, we found that we were paying women well and on a par with the men. I wrote a note on this as part of my learning notes to all employees, and I was amazed that so many managers told me that their mothers, wives, etc., said to them how proud they were of PepsiCo and that this was a fair place for rewarding talent.

Fairness also depends on whether you are showcasing your team's talent to your boss. Every team member wants to feel that his work in a company is recognized at the highest levels. When this is done regularly, the engagement and commitment of employees are much better.

Fairness is about giving credit where it is due. I remember that I used to make slides for my director, Anand Bhatia, when I was a brand manager in Hindustan Lever. It was amazing that he would call me from Delhi or London or Mumbai after the presentation to tell me that it went well and that I had done a good job of the slide-making process. It was a small thing, but it made me work so much more for his success. We own up to our success, we own up to our subordinates' success—we also need to own up and contribute to our boss's success and failure.

Former US secretary of defence Robert McNamara described the situation when President Kennedy was getting brickbats for the Bay of Pigs disaster. This was the solution suggested by McNamara. He told President Kennedy that he was willing to go before the media and confess that the whole thing was his idea and plan. To which President Kennedy said, 'It was your plan, Robert, but I approved it when I could have rejected it, and hence I must face the music/brickbats.' McNamara writes, 'I decided that day that I will be fully loyal to Kennedy and his family.' That's a great story on fairness. Clearly, fairness wins you loyalty.

Being Consistent

I think leaders are inherently inconsistent if they don't have a strong true north. A true north derives from the behaviour you exhibit in practising your personal value system and your commitment to your company's values. A good example is collaboration. Every leader claims that they are collaborative but in reality they are not. They are collaborative when it suits them.

Consistency does not mean saying yes or saying no all the time.

Consistency simply means that given the same set of data, you would come to the same answer or decision. Consistent decisions are seen as fair and accurate. When you are consistent, your team will trust you to do the right thing.

This is very important when we judge people and their potential. I had this funny experience when one of the people reporting to me didn't like the work of an HR manager and wanted to pull down his rating. We pushed back, and the HR manager got a good rating. We were all surprised when in six months' time the same manager wanted to promote this HR manager. Everyone involved in the process was flabbergasted at this inconsistency.

When you are consistent, you take the guesswork out of your team and the system. Your team will not be worried about the boss's mood, etc., before approaching you. When you are consistent, you are like the sun to your team. Everyone knows when the sun rises and when it sets, and everyone makes plans around that. The same will happen in your team, and you will get speed like never before. Leaders inspire confidence with their consistency.

Inconsistency breeds insecurity in a team and organization. A leader's consistency comes from his/her core values, their ability to communicate and connect, and their ability to explain when there is a debate on consistency in the organization.

A good example of inconsistency in strategy and its communication is Nokia and its approach to the Android platform. Nokia pooh-poohed it to start with, then went with Windows and then reversed its decision and went the Android way, and then reversed again. This was inconsistency of the highest order from the board and the CEO, and it created huge insecurity in the organization, which eventually led to its acquisition and then decline.

Leaders cannot be inconsistent about strategy and direction.

Leaders are seen as inconsistent when they play games with their subordinates and peer group. Politics of any kind takes away from one's consistency in trying to achieve the best results for the organization.

Being consistent also makes you predictable on a few issues, and I have seen that helps build trust. I talk to the sixty managers who are my direct reports, and to their reports, every fortnight for 10–15 minutes in one-on-one conversations. I consistently look for the consistency of their messaging. Some tend to overplay situations, some tend to underplay situations, but over a period of time I have understood who is consistent and who isn't. This is what people who work with us do, too.

Consistency also requires a cool head. I once asked the cricketer Ricky Ponting whom he would send out to bat if his life depended on it. He thought for a while and said, 'Steve Waugh . . . Waugh had a steely determination and was level-headed.'

Every organization wants steely-headed, level-headed, cool-headed men and women.

Being a Coach

Every team leader is a coach. He/she is a coach through their actions, behaviour, words. In a fast-changing world, where employees don't have the time for development programmes, the best development is the way their leader coaches them. You coach people in the time they work with you and help them set out on their journeys to their respective dreams.

Sixty-six per cent of millennials expect their team leader to develop and coach them to the next level. That's a scary expectation of team leaders.

Every member in your team looks up to you for coaching. This is even more true when you are leading CEOs and senior managers in regional roles or head office conglomerate roles. As a leader, it is my job to coach functional heads for business acumen, because in the end a business wins and not a function. You have to have something to offer people who work with you. It can be discipline, it can be aggression, it can be attitude, it can be structural thinking, it can be having fun. But you need to recognize that you have something of value to offer your team.

As a team leader, you need to believe in your team, you need to have faith, you need to treat each one differently. In the early days when I was a team leader, I thought consistency was about being the same with every member of my team, and I then realized that it was a mistake. While you share many things with the full team, you need to coach each one a bit differently. You need to give some people some tailwind, you need to give some people the challenge to do better. As a coach, you need to keep the emotion aside and take decisions for furthering the careers of people. If emotion gets in the way, you cannot be a good coach.

How Team Communication Has Changed

Team Communication Has Become Faster → Comfortable Collaboration → Increasing Team Morale → Remote Control

More Instant Access ← Sales Coaching Using Real Conversations ← Decentralization and Flattening ← Getting off of Email

Source: https://www.forbes.com/sites/forbesbusinessdevelopmentcouncil/2018/08/02/10-ways-technology-has-changed-teamcommunication/?sh=47df83067cb4

Every team leader needs coaching too, and it can come from your own team member. You can, as a team leader, get coached by someone experienced in your team. After a frustrating day of trying to set fair targets with my area sales managers at Hindustan Lever's Chennai branch, I was frustrated and took the old lion of the Chennai branch, 'Laks' (Lakshmanan), out for a drink. He had his whisky and I my lime juice. I asked Laks about the day. He was merciless—he said it was a terrible meeting, he was trying to get everyone to agree with the targets and no one was agreeing. He said, 'You are the boss, Shiv. You have to make up your mind and tell us our targets and how to do them. Your style of selling a target democratically will never work. Maybe think of coaching us about execution of the target.' That was valuable advice from Laks.

Over the years, I have realized that getting 60 per cent agreement and 100 per cent commitment from a team is more important than 100 per cent agreement and 0 per cent commitment.

The key to coaching a team is enabling them to achieve more than their potential. When you are a good team, the competition is yourself.

Football has a great lesson for us. Football fans are fanatics—they stay with the same club as loyal supporters for years, either because they were born somewhere near the club or because they adopted the club as an outlet for their dreams.

Jose Mourinho, the legendary football coach, says that fans love the club but could hate the team from time to time. They want to see the team represent the values the club stands for. And above all, the fans want to see the team give their best day in and day out. When they see that their team is not trying hard enough, they fall out of love with the team.

At the football club Manchester United, there is a plaque that reads, 'At Manchester United we strive for perfection and if we fail we might just have to settle for excellence.'

A good coach sets high expectations. That's his/her job.

I feel many of us have low expectations of our teams, when our job is to make them think bigger, better, smarter. This low expectation becomes a challenge in the way we coach them. I have always had high expectations from every team I led, big or small. When you are the best team, like Nokia India was, you have reached the top of the mountain, and others are hungry to get there, to take you down. You are your own enemy and can fall down.

As a coach of a successful team, you have to set newer measures to beat others and get better. When Phil Jackson came to coach the Chicago Bulls and the legendary Michael Jordan, he told Jordan, 'I can't teach you basketball, but I can make you a better basketballer.' Jackson then focused on measures like assists, blocks, etc., to give Jordan's game an all-round appeal, and Jordan went on to win many Most Valuable Player awards during that partnership with Jackson.

In organizations, leaders tend to get their teams to focus on other teams that sit around them, and they build an illusion of superiority by comparing them against an average pool.

I have always coached my teams to think at an absolute level: Are we better than the best in the industry? Are we industry-beating as a team?

I find that the best moments to coach are during failure, when something has gone wrong, the market share is down, a presentation didn't go well, a product launch bombed. These are pivotal coaching moments, as long as you, as a coach, are willing to be forthright and yet supportive, and to chart a new course. Whenever my team has a failure, I always start by asking them what went right and what we could have done better. That dialogue has helped the team and me immensely.

The US Navy SEALs have an expression: 'Hold fast, stay true.' This is a marine expression, when the ship goes through turbulence and you cannot navigate looking for the stars in the sky with waves all around you. The people on the ship have to hold fast to whatever is close by, and the captain of the ship has to stay true to the direction.

Coaching involves positive strokes and feedback. Feedback is the breakfast of champions—some thrive on it, many don't. Many managers get soft in their head and want to hear only good things after they have crossed middle management. Having an honest feedback session with them is a real problem. Sometimes, feedback starts bugging the recipient and he/she starts resenting you. A good coaching strategy in such cases is to step back and let the person be, since you are not getting through anyway. I feel that in some cases, people hate help, and they need to recognize areas of improvement themselves.

Managing Prima Donnas and Weight-Carriers

Every team has great people, and in comparison to those great people others might look regular. In a team which has Sachin Tendulkar, most batsmen will look regular. In a movie that has Amitabh Bachchan, most of the cast will look regular. As team leaders, we need the prima donna as much as we need the regular talented person. There are times when the organization panders to the prima donna, and there are instances when it's time to pull the plug on the prima donna.

Let's consider what's happened with Virat Kohli quitting the Test captaincy. The Board of Control for Cricket in India (BCCI) accepted Kohli's decision and was willing to move on. In 2017, the BCCI had backed Kohli over Kumble in their conflict regarding team discipline and Kumble's plain-speak to bowlers. Times change.

Conflict within a Team Is Essential

A certain amount of 'creative abrasion' allows a team to identify alternative approaches. However, everyone must agree that conflicts won't get personal and promise to surface the reasons behind their disagreements.

Image source: https://www.freepik.com/
Source: https://www.inc.com/geoffrey-james/10-surprising-scientific-facts-aboutteams.html

Once someone asked Imran Khan, the erstwhile cricket captain and now the prime minister of Pakistan, how he managed a bunch of different people, talented, corrupt, undisciplined, etc. Imran's answer was simple: 'I pick the players who I believe have the best potential to make Pakistan win. I am not concerned about their other activities. I am not giving my children in marriage to them. I treat them for their talent on the day.'

Another good example is what Alex Ferguson did with Ronaldo when he was the manager of Manchester United. He sold Ronaldo for $80 million to Real Madrid at the peak of Ronaldo's ability, because he felt it was best for both Ronaldo and Manchester United.

I believe that a good way to think of a team and its capabilities is to think of it as a room where the ceiling is the prima donnas and the floor is the weight-carriers in the organization. The weight-carriers are the foundation of the organization, they understand the processes, they understand how work happens in the organization. Without the weight-carriers, the organization will come to a grinding halt.

The trick for a leader is to grow both the prima donnas and the weight-carriers in the same ratio, at the same pace, so that the gap between them is reduced or maintained. If the gap between the prima donna and the rest widens, it creates strife, insecurity, dependence and lopsided rewards in the organization. No team can excel with prima donnas alone; it needs the regular guys/gals to fill many roles. The New Zealand cricket team is a great example of zero prima donnas but consistent excellent results. I feel this is a basic lesson for the BCCI and the Indian cricket team.

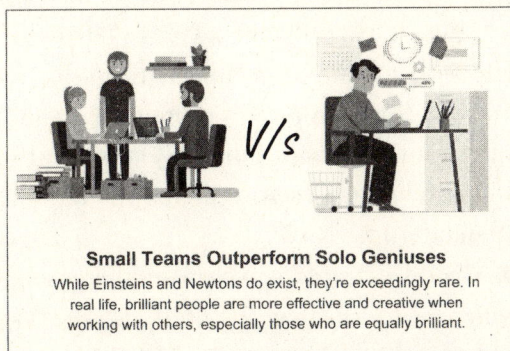

Small Teams Outperform Solo Geniuses
While Einsteins and Newtons do exist, they're exceedingly rare. In real life, brilliant people are more effective and creative when working with others, especially those who are equally brilliant.

Image source: https://www.freepik.com/
Source: https://www.inc.com/geoffrey-james/10-surprising-scientific-facts-about-teams.html

GE had a rule where every year they would take out the bottom 5 per cent of managers in a forced-ranking method. I always disagreed with this method. My premise was that if

GE was hiring well and spending enough time getting the intake right, it was their job to make people perform to their potential. By force ranking, GE lost many good managers over the years. Ideally, GE should have also got rid of the manager of the manager and the HR person responsible, because they hadn't done their job. There is no end to this madness, and I am happy to see that many organizations are doing away with the bell curve for assessment.

I think the newer generation of employees will not accept the prima donna and weight-carrier labels. In a start-up culture, the owner is the prima donna, and everyone else is a weight-carrier. I think the work world will need to think of newer ways to manage high-value talent and core-capability talent.

By definition, the prima donnas are a challenge to manage. Here are some ways to think about managing them:

1. The prima donnas are normally full of themselves and in a hurry to get from one role to another in a jiffy. They feel constrained if they spend too much time in a role and worry they could lose their prima-donna status.

2. The prima donnas have a higher hunger for achievement compared to the normal person in your organization. As a leader, try and stoke that achievement-orientation but without comparing them to the others in the team.

3. Set a new, higher benchmark for the prima donna. The prima donna repeatedly will want you to

compare his or her output with the average person's, and you should not fall into that trap. You have to ask and demand a higher standard from the prima donna.

4. Stoke the prima donna's ego when needed. They react to that well.

5. Set upper and lower limits in dealing with the prima donnas. If there is no upper limit, then you will end up bending over backwards to please every prima donna, and that will become the norm for everyone in the organization.

6. The prima donnas will never understand a fair leader to start with. I have been lucky to work with so many talented people. More than seventy people who worked with me went on to be CXOs and CEOs of good-sized organizations. They saw my initial chats with them about standards, performance, organization agenda and values as hot air, and only later, when they became CEOs, did they realize what I was trying to do. One of them called me a few years ago and said, 'I thought it was something you were saying for effect. Now I realize the sincerity and commitment behind what you were doing with us as a team.'

Managing teams in a successful organization is different from managing teams when the organization is under pressure. In good times, Nokia had a fabulous culture—forgiving, mistakes were seen as learning opportunities, etc.

When Nokia started floundering, one began to see inter-team rivalry, intra-team rivalry, and everyone was insecure almost every day, fearing the worst. Anyone who was from the old team was seen as pedestrian, and anyone who had come in with the new team was seen as a saviour.

I tried my best to be authentic and honest and fair in that dark Nokia period, when I led emerging markets, and I can say that the multinational and multicultural team we had in Dubai imploded with insecurity.

This was a direct result of what they were seeing and hearing across the world. Every question in a meeting was seen as a threat, every suggestion was viewed with scepticism. There was large-scale downsizing, and the organization was the poorer for talent, starved for diversity and bankrupt in terms of inclusion. It started with the team management of the CEOs executive team.

A lot of first-time CEOs ask me if they should be close or distant with their teams and the organization. I always ask them to be authentic, to be who they are and connect with people the way they normally would. You cannot fake emotion in a team.

As a leader, be generous in your praise of the team and give them all the credit when things go well. This is not easily done by leaders. For example, when Imran Khan delivered his speech after winning the World Cup in 1992, a lot of it was about the cancer hospital in his mother's memory. He forgot to thank his own team for their success. People remember these things long after the event. Imran Khan was a terrific captain, but at that moment he forgot to thank his team enough. Simply unpardonable.

The other measure of a true team leader is the way the leader handles bad news. PepsiCo leaders were very poor at handling bad news that came up the line. It could also be because PepsiCo was more of an execution-focused company as opposed to being a strategy-led company.

When you, as a leader, don't take bad news well, people stop giving you bad news, and the culture becomes a rah-rah culture where everything is like you're in paradise—in full bloom and doing well. In such companies, bad news comes to the leader through the grapevine or through vested interests in the company, and that creates its own politics.

When I listen to bad news I always ask myself what we could have done to avoid it, what we have learnt from it and how we will ensure that we don't repeat the same thing. If it's a genuine mistake, then I tend to move ahead quickly. If it happened due to a lack of effort and basics, then I do have a serious conversation with the concerned people.

Our biggest failure in Nokia was when we launched the first dual sim, and Kaustav Chatterjee was leading the product-launch efforts. This launch was a miserable failure, and in a week we knew that we were in trouble. The team was distraught. They had done all they could, but the technology of call transfer, on which we based this model, did not work in small towns and rural areas. We had tested the feature in urban markets, where it worked well, and assumed that it would work in rural markets.

We gave the team a standing ovation when we reviewed the launch—because they had done what was in their hands—

gave them a bottle of champagne and asked them to go out and have a good meal.

Raman Singh, current CHRO, ABB, is an ex-PepsiCo person. He introduced a Learning from Failure award at PepsiCo and nominated himself for the first award. Admitting failure on a leader's part galvanizes the team and makes them want to do better in order not to let you down.

I have learnt that sharing vulnerability with a team is good practice for a leader. It makes the leader so much more real and look like a normal human being for the team.

A good leader and a good team can achieve a lot. In the future, both of them need to trust each other, build their combined capability at work be on a relentless path of capability improvement and deliver impactfully.

K.K. Sridhar

K.K. Sridhar was my boss and friend at Unilever and one of the most versatile leaders. Sridhar worked in Unilever and SC Johnson and Sons Inc. He has worked across three continents in customer management, global sales transformation, global mergers and acquisitions. Sridhar is a certified coach and has studied in IIM Ahmedabad.

In this interview Sridhar talks about managing people from different cultures, managing sales teams and marketing teams, managing high-energy brand managers and handling difficult subordinates. He emphasizes the role of listening as a skill and coaching teams. He is a great coach.

As a team leader, you have led consumer-facing teams, marketing teams and business teams. How does managing a team change over these three domains?

At the outset, I learnt very early on that people management is a fundamental skill you need to advance in your career.

When you treat people with dignity, respect and tact, even the most challenging person becomes collaborative. Also, I am inspired by the Ubuntu philosophy (it's an ethnic tribe in South Africa): 'I am who I am because of who we all collectively are.' 'If you want to go fast, go alone. But if you want to go farther in life, then you have to go together.' This philosophy has always guided me in the way I manage teams. I've always seen myself as a facilitator. I very rarely have had to use overt power or authority to manage my teams. I've done it mostly through positive influence, appealing to the hearts and minds, evoking the right emotions, motivation and getting people aligned to a common cause.

Irrespective of which team you are managing, there is no cookie-cutter formula that will apply in all situations, because it calls for situational leadership. Depending on the issue that each team is facing at a particular point in time in the business cycle, I would adapt my leadership style to get the best results in that situation.

Three things are common about managing teams: Clarity with regard to the stakeholders, shared vision and goal, and empowerment. We need clarity on who the primary and secondary stakeholders are, and on their expectations. Envisioning the stakeholders this way gives you a sense of direction, helps you assess the resources needed and appropriate time allocation in order to deliver according to their expectations.

The second common feature is that every team must have a measurable goal to accomplish. And these goals must flow from a 'co-created' vision. You want the team's buy-in before getting them to sign up. You do it by going to them with a draft vision and incorporating their inputs to sharpen it. If they can see their thumbprint, it results in high commitment.

The third common feature has to do with empowerment. If they feel empowered, they take ownership, become more creative, more self-confident and more self-accountable, as opposed to assigning blame.

Talking of differences, the role of sales is lead generation, that of marketing is demand generation, while business teams pull all functions together to deliver financial results.

Other differences relate to the primary stakeholders and KPIs [key performance indicators]. For a customer-facing team, the primary stakeholder is the customer; for a marketing team, it's the consumer; for a business team, it is the shareholders and the board. The KPIs for the sales manager are sales volume and value, distribution width and depth, share of shelf, merchandizing, trade spend, etc. In the case of marketing, KPIs will be category growth, share of category, the number of new products launched, speed to market, revenue from NPDs, etc. The business team, on the other hand, is looking at top-line revenue growth, gross margin, overheads, bottom-line profit growth and return on assets.

Managing teams in these three domains calls for an agile and adaptable leadership style and knowledge of what will motivate them. Sales teams tend to have a mix of stalwarts rooted in tradition and youngsters who bring in youthful energy and new thinking. I would respect the experience and stability provided by the veterans while offering challenging learning opportunities for the youngsters to contribute to modern and novel channels and grow. I would like them to benefit from the cross-pollination, so that they together succeed as a team and work well with marketing. I would encourage and support the marketing teams that have youngsters bustling with ideas to take calculated risks and learn from these. I promote the mantra, 'Experiment a lot, fail cheap and learn a lot.' I would promote seamless working with agency and media partners externally, and with R&D, supply chain and sales internally. Being multifunctional, business teams need a high degree of cross-collaboration, mutual trust and interdependence to deliver successfully on a co-created vision and unified objective.

One of the challenges that people in authority face has to do with coming across as the boss's man rather than a leader. How did you handle this challenge?

My mental model is to be a good team player and be committed to achieving business results. When the business sets a target, I ask myself the following questions: Do I believe it is achievable? Do I have a plan to achieve it? What additional resources do I need? If I have concerns that it might be unrealistic, I develop a logic-driven case with options and address these with my boss in private, align on resources needed and walk out with a unified objective. I would never say to my team, 'My boss is pushing this target on me.' On the contrary, I take ownership of it. In a two-way conversation, one of us persuades the other. So, once aligned,

I would say to my team, 'This is what the business needs to achieve. And here are the reasons why we need to do this. I am committed because I believe we can do it together.' And I will encourage the team to ask questions. At times I have said, 'If we don't achieve it, we will become a smaller business than what we were last year. And I'm sure none of you want to be part of a smaller business.' So, you set the agenda.

Another challenge for a supervisor, especially when they're in the sales team, is how to build a team where all members are essentially competing against one another? What do you do in that case?

Sales managers tend to be competitive and like to win, given the DNA of the function. However, in line with the Ubuntu philosophy, my message to the team unequivocally is to focus on 'how we can collectively make it happen'. So, the emphasis is on team achievement, not on competing with one another unhealthily for individual glory. An individual star shining while the team fails is unproductive. In cricket, if a star player keeps scoring centuries while the team loses, it is not a contribution to be proud of. It is about elevating them to be a high-performance team and rewarding the team and not individual stars.

And a high-performance team, I would remind them, has a clear shared purpose and alignment, a shared leadership and interdependence built on mutual trust. I will tell them, 'I am a facilitator, but you are leaders in your own right. This is a trust-based environment providing psychological safety. If you disagree here, no issues. But I don't want you to walk out of the room with a disagreement unresolved. Let's resolve it right now.'

The other thing I do is to observe behaviour patterns. I have a pretty good idea about the personality types in my team. I know there is a guy who always comes up with a crazy question. I'll speak to him prior to the meeting and say, 'You always come up with some offbeat ideas. What do you have for this meeting?' It's about giving respect and valuing the other person as an equal team member.

Sometimes, teams that come from different cultures have to work together. You have handled Indian teams, Dutch teams, American teams. How do you vary your personal style to manage such culturally diverse teams?

Teams are made of people, and people's basic human traits are the same, regardless of nationality, colour and culture. What drives them towards success is the same thing—whether you're American, Dutch, Brazilian or Chinese—you want to grow, learn, get promoted, get recognized for good performance, make an impact. However, the way they receive and process information is different. In India, for example, we deal with ambiguity better than anybody else in the world, because we are brought up in a chaotic environment. So, we always improvise, have a workaround. In Western culture, they find dealing with ambiguity challenging. They've got a very structured line of thought, consistent with their local ecosystem. Hence, a structured approach with defined processes works well.

I learnt to manage the Chinese team differently from how I would manage an Indian, American, Latin American or European team. Instead of giving them an open field, I found they thrived as flawless implementers when they were given clear directions. However, in the Western and Latin American world, people are more vocal. Therefore, you must remain open-minded for your draft ideas to be modified before implementation. In Asian cultures, building relationships precedes tasks, while in Western cultures, tasks come ahead. In Asian cultures, context is important, while in other cultures it is not.

One needs to figure out how to connect with teams emotionally. Using the sports metaphor works, e.g., cricket in South Asia, basketball or football or baseball in the US, soccer, rugby in Europe and Latin America. I follow popular sports of various countries and their heroes to keep myself informed. In summary, I remain open-minded and change my style in a culturally relevant manner to be effective.

How about troublemakers? How do you handle an argumentative subordinate who goes into a second-decimal argument or that undisciplined sales manager who never comes prepared for meetings?

If there is a pattern of someone not coming prepared for the meetings, obviously, you've got to talk to them one-on-one, but not in front of the others. Make them aware of how their tardiness impacts the team productivity negatively. I will ask them questions to make them reflect: How did you perform in the meeting? How do you think your session went? How could you have contributed more? And nine out of ten times, I found that when you ask somebody to reflect and hold a mirror to them, they realize that they did a shoddy job, need to improve and do better at the next meeting. Those who are not able to reflect, you've got to really tell them 'like it is', but respectfully, and set up a time-bound development plan with markers.

It is important to identify the team members who think differently. I don't brand them as dissenters. I would encourage them to voice their opinions constructively, because they may have some valid new perspectives which could help the team arrive at a better solution. Shutting them up is not a good idea. My communication to such team members is, 'If you feel you have a different point of view, which will build on our discussions and improve the quality of our collective decision, please share it.' If the rest of the team don't respond to the idea very enthusiastically, people are smart and realize themselves. I would use this as a teaching moment and meet them later one-on-one, and ask them to reflect: 'You had a chance to voice your idea. What do you think happened?' They become far less argumentative as a result.

Speaking of bad fish, how do you pull up an underperformer in a team, someone who is hurting the overall team performance, without breaking their confidence?

In a team review of progress vs targets/objectives, I would share a traffic-light report. The colour code is green for those who are on target, amber for those who are close to the target but have minor issues, and red for those who have lagged behind/missed the target and have big issues. When you flash the traffic-light report on a screen in a community of peers, nobody wants a red colour against their region or name.

Typically, in a group meeting, I would ask, 'What are the top three things you would do to move from red to amber, and from amber to green? What help do you need?' Redirect the conversation to solution-seeking as opposed to talking about the problems and getting mired in endless discussions. Focus the discussion on finding a solution, even if it is not a perfect solution. You're changing the mental gears of the person when you move from talking about a problem to finding a solution. Even the most pessimistic guy in such a situation will start thinking of a solution.

If someone is a consistent underperformer, I would meet with them one-on-one. I would listen to their analysis, understand the reasons, ask them for a plan to plug the gaps and direct the conversation to an aligned series of next steps. Also, I would provide resources if legitimately required. Additionally, I would make them aware that continued underperformance won't be acceptable.

Are there any lessons that you draw in managing a team from sports?

Sports offer us valuable leadership lessons—be it cricket or soccer or basketball. In cricket, I am particularly inspired by M.S. Dhoni's leadership traits, which are relevant to being an authentic business leader. He is a great role model for staying true to himself, leading from the front, empowering his team, handling success and failure with equanimity, being a great team player after stepping down from captaincy, empowering his team and showing faith in their abilities. You've heard a lot of his players say M.S. Dhoni always tries to raise the errant players, he doesn't try to put them down.

What according to you is a good team?

As Simon Sinek says: 'A team is not a group of people who work together. A team is a group of people who trust each other.' A good team is one that is made up of ordinary individuals delivering extraordinary results. If you have a team full of stars, sometimes that team can underperform, compared to a team of ordinary individuals. So, a good team is one which has a clear vision and a shared commitment, which has mutual trust, interdependence and reliability, which has members who support one another and deliver the results . . . We all know every team is only as good as its weakest link. We can't afford to have a weak link.

What is the role of symbols and symbolism in building teams? I remember you'd made a Top Guns forum when you ran a customer-facing team?

I think people connect emotionally to symbols and metaphors much better than to words. When I was leading a team at Lipton, inspired by the US Navy Strike Fighter

Tactics Instructor programme, I created a group, in the pre-cellphone era, called 'Top Guns', for those who met their targets consistently. We invited the Top Guns to a meeting at the headquarters, got them to meet the CEO and asked each of them to share their experiences. We recorded this and circulated the video for dissemination through various regional meetings. This became highly inspirational, and everybody wanted to be a part of the Top Gun Club, because only the best could join it. It was all about raising their aspirations and their game.

C.V.L. Srinivas

CVL is the country manager of WPP India, responsible for all WPP entities in the country. He has twenty-five years of experience in media and advertising. He is a proven leader, with a track record in transforming companies, nurturing talent, media management, partnerships, mobile marketing and go-to-market strategies. CVL is a cool, balanced professional whose word matters in the media and advertising business.

In this interview he talks about the challenges of building a team of superstars, getting alignment, and being both an ambassador of the global company and a leader of the country.

Through your career, you have been a part of historic teams, like Fulcrum, and of teams that didn't do much. What according to you are the ingredients of a great team and a weak/poor team? What is the role of the leader in a good team and in a bad team? And

what is the role of followers when they have a bad team leader?

I don't think there is anything like a weak team or a good team. One of my big learnings as a leader is that everyone has strengths and some shortcomings. The job of a leader is to harness the strengths of people in his/her team and support them to work on their weaknesses.

The responsibility of a team's success or failure is collective, although I feel a leader needs to stick his/her neck out and back his team in the event of failure. Without failures there is no success, and without trying there is no failure. The role of a leader in a good team is to not get in the way of individual brilliance but look at ways of connecting the dots and gaining more value collectively. Empowerment is critical, and there should be no insecurities of any kind in anyone who is part of the team, including the leader.

When a team is not performing to its full potential, the first important step is for the team to collectively realize that they can do better. The role of a leader is to encourage objectivity, look within and get feedback on his/her leadership style, the role clarity among members and issues being faced by them. In most cases, the factors affecting team performance are controllable. It is important to create an open environment where issues can be discussed and resolved.

When followers have a bad team leader, eventually one or some of them tend to take on larger roles and become the go-to leaders for the rest. Bad leaders generally don't last very long; if they do, good teams will not stay together.

You have been a part of large established entities and also a part of a start-up. How do teams in large companies compare with those in small companies? What are the big differences?

Teams in smaller companies often tend to be a lot more cohesive and very naturally come together without the need for processes and protocols. Teams in larger companies must be brought together in most cases, especially if it is a matrix organization. The role of a leader is to make it worthwhile for teams across the different units of the company to collaborate and work for their collective benefit.

In smaller companies, you often must make do with what you have. As a team you try much harder to succeed. This is typical of underdog teams—they have amazing resilience and take on audacious goals. In larger companies with set processes, it becomes harder to take risks. Here again the role of the leader is to create an environment that encourages an entrepreneurial approach. This can be done by empowering people, cutting down levels of hierarchy, simplifying processes, creating shadow boards with youngsters, etc.

In smaller companies, individual brilliance stands out more easily, and people often tend to become superstars very quickly. It is important to recognize such talent and support them as they grow within the ranks of the organization, so that teams can be built around them, and this can help the organization scale effectively. In larger organizations this is much harder to do and often gets missed due to the sheer number of people. It is therefore very important for leaders to devise ways of spotting talent within their organization across levels, and to ensure they are motivated to stay the course and help transform the company.

You currently lead WPP in India in one of its most important markets. You lead, formally and informally, a bunch of star CEOs and business leaders. How do you manage such a star team? What is your style of communicating with them, and what do you focus on?

What I enjoy most in my current role is the people I work with. I cannot add any value to what each of them does, since they are all superstars in their own fields. My job is to bring people together to collectively benefit our clients and our opcos [operating companies]. As long as this understanding is clear and established, there are no issues whatsoever.

We support our opcos to win in the market by focusing on areas where we are better off as one company . . . To be able to efficiently and effectively implement this strategy across the wider company, we have internal communities, like the Client–Leader Community, the Technology Innovation Group, People Forum, Stella, Green Team, etc., which act as connectors. We have representation from across our opcos in all the communities and a designated leader.

As for communication, while there are formal and structured sessions, like our CEO meetings, where we share updates at a company level, best practices across opcos and get feedback on various things, we have tried to create a very open atmosphere, resulting in a lot more frequent interactions. This has been especially so in the last eighteen months, when we were all jointly managing the COVID situation.

As a team leader, how do you strike a balance between small talk, personal talk and business talk when you deal with your team?

As a team leader, it is important to communicate frequently. I guess each leader has his/her own style. For me, it is a combination of structured team meetings to keep track of our business, people issues, etc., combined with one-on-one interactions for the so-called small talk and personal talk. It's important for leaders to show empathy towards their immediate team members and share some of their own challenges to help create a feeling of trust and openness.

In your current job there is the risk of being seen as a headquarters man driving the HQ's agenda. How do you handle this?

The role of the leader is to build trust with both his team and the HQ, so that he can openly communicate on both sides. This is done by being open and transparent about issues that crop up, and by presenting facts and data to back a certain point. Once trust is established, even difficult conversations can be managed to balance both local and global points of view.

Digital technology is disrupting your industry. How do you prepare your team and ecosystem for that?

We do this through various initiatives. We have created a Technology Innovation Group (TIG) that has the best tech minds from across our various opcos. We delve into various areas where technology is transforming marketing and drive programmes across the company.

We promote individual champions and teams in certain specific areas and get them to build communities across the company, as we have done in voice tech and other emerging areas.

We have an active partner programme, with both global and local tech and data players, and co-create solutions for our clients by working across our different opcos. We focus on L&D to upskill our people; this happens both at individual opcos and through programmes run more centrally. There are a lot of initiatives being run globally as well, which our people have access to, including WPP OPEN, where we have democratized data and tech across the company.

COVID has created a big disruption. How did you manage the results in such a year, and what did you tell your team through the year? Did you have a fixed plan, a quarter-by-quarter plan? How did you keep the engagement up in this period?

Right from when the pandemic struck, the priority was to take care of our people and their families. We got a lot of support from HQ and were able to support our people through various services. We set up teleconsulting with medical experts, ambulance on call, a helpline for medical supplies, oxygen concentrators and kicked off a vaccination drive across all our offices. We have frequent communication within the company at the leadership level, within opcos and town halls across the company, including with our global CEO. We organize frequent sessions for all our people and their families with doctors, mental health experts and others to provide information and clear their doubts about COVID and its aftereffects.

When it came to business, the focus was more on the here and now—ensuring that our services to clients did not get disrupted. We dialled up our engagement with clients by communicating across levels and worked jointly to manage the crisis.

How is managing your team in a virtual world different from managing your team in a physical world?

We need to be much more flexible in the virtual world. We need to recognize that most people are facing challenges, and adapt meeting times, duration and participation to accommodate for this. With no constraints of travel or location, one can afford to reach out to a wider set of people, make meetings a lot more inclusive, provide more opportunities for branches to work with the central teams, etc. This can be fully leveraged to build a more inclusive culture in the company.

One can do more meetings in a given day and enhance the quality of interactions by keeping in touch with the team members on topics of mutual interest, beyond the routine discussions. One must encourage people to reach out for support, and begin each call by discussing the situation, how each one is doing or what they are picking up from colleagues. One must encourage people to take breaks, maintain a discipline of work hours and not disturb them on weekends. Working in a virtual world can be more productive, but it needs to be balanced with giving your team members space and being empathetic to their feelings.

How do you as a leader challenge a star who doesn't deliver results in your team?

Try to understand what is preventing him/her from delivering. If it is something controllable, try and work things out and give the person more time. If it is a case of the person losing motivation, encourage them by reminding them of their own stellar performances, giving them more 'open' recognition and arranging for support. If the person is looking for newer challenges and is bored with the present job, expand the scope of the job. It is important to address the issue within a timeframe. Sometimes it may be better for the person to take a break and come back refreshed.

You have a number of women in your team. What qualities make women good team players?

We are fortunate to have a fair number of women leaders in our team. They bring a very balanced approach to problem-solving, and are extremely diligent and very caring about the larger organization and our people. They are all very accomplished in their respective fields, and it is really inspiring to be a part of such a team.

Nisha Narayanan

Nisha is the director and COO of Red FM and Magic FM. She has over twenty years of experience in the broadcast media industry. Nisha is passionate, creative, full of ideas and has high energy levels. She is also known for the outstanding collection of saris that she has.

In this interview she talks about the energy needed to manage a team in a daily-market-share business, how to handle the prima donnas and how to translate ideas into action.

Your radio business is a daily-market-share business. How do you ensure that there is enough energy in the team every day? Does it come from you, from a few members or from all?

I focus a lot on the kind of team we have built over a period of time, and we are constantly looking for people who are self-starters—very passionately driven people. For me, personally, the energy comes from the fact that every day there is always a challenge to take up. So we're always pushing the envelope, we are thinking out of the box, we are taking a lot of risks. And because there is a risk, especially during the pandemic, you know you wake up trying to find a solution. So, for me, innovation is key. I think the business thrives on innovation. And when I say innovation, taking risks, thinking out of the box, challenging yourself, all of that comes into play. We have people who take risks, think differently, are very passionate, etc.

Once you put together that environment, you'll end up creating very high-energy stuff. We're constantly on the move. And I can say that it flows from the top all the way to the last mile within the team. We're constantly doing multiple things . . .

The beauty of creativity comes out even more if you take risks, challenge the norms, think differently and come up with fresh thoughts . . . I think that's where the energy flows from. You're always enthusiastic; you wake up in the morning and think, 'Okay, I've not done this before. Let me try and do that.' So, from the sound engineer and producer to the creative guy and the RJ, from the business level to the marketing person, the energy flows through, because they are all constantly challenged.

When I listen to the radio, I only listen to the RJ. The marketing, the sound engineers and even you, for that matter, are all invisible to me. How often do you have to intervene in what I hear on a daily basis?

I am an extremely hands-on person. As part of the work, of course, we look after all departments, but I sit with the marketing, programming and creative teams personally. And I challenge them, because when you are a creative person, you end up churning very similar ideas day after day. You get into that form, that habit of coming up with a similar thought process. One of the things I constantly push these teams to do is to just say, 'No, I don't like it.' So they need to keep convincing me about why a certain idea is different.

For me, the energy comes from taking risks and pushing the norms. And because I do that, the team is compelled to keep pace with me. We sort of egg each other on and push each other to be very competitive. My operating style carries a lot of personal touch . . . We have an open-door policy— teams can walk in, they can discuss a lot of things. It's not hierarchical. I also encourage people who are fresh in the system to come and share their ideas, etc. And what I try to do is to solve problems for them and just make their life a little easier . . .

How do you manage talent in your team?

Talent-mapping is a science in itself . . . If you are able to sit with your team, have conversations, start listening to them and start appreciating them, I think that's 50 per cent of the work done, because many times creative teams feel upset when they're not heard . . . It's about giving a personal touch to creative talent. And I would say not just creative teams but anybody who's doing well, whether in sales, marketing, digital—what they need is a personal touch, or personal encouragement and appreciation.

Are there times when there is a clash of ideas, when the creative guy comes up with something and you have to take a back seat?

In our working environment at Radio One, one has to give a lot of liberty for creative work. And we should allow that to happen. So, in fact, I encourage them to think more creatively, and we don't control them. There is a certain framework that I work within. And I tell them, that's your playing field. So as long as you're not deviating too much from that, I am okay. However, because some of them really love taking risks, 80 per cent of the time they would come up with another idea which goes beyond the boundary as well. That is when probably some other considerations about the business and brand come into play. Many times, the big superstars generate a lot of excitement by doing something completely new and fresh. I think we should allow that, because when the superstars do it, it encourages newer talent to also emulate them.

How has the pandemic changed your approach to managing a team?

Because of the pandemic, unfortunately, we had to take some administrative decisions, which means that today, we're far leaner. But that also means that now, every single person in the team is far more empowered, far more responsible to take a decision on their own. They've got more responsibilities. So that, I think, is a very critical thing, because suddenly there's a lot of growth for them as well. And more responsibility. Parallelly, we push most of them to put on the entrepreneurial cap. You know, it's one thing to be a salaried employee and quite another to put on the entrepreneurial cap . . .

The personal touch and connection with the teams have increased manyfold now. The radio business in itself is something which is very high on micromanagement. But the micromanagement has also increased tremendously. And the pandemic has also taught us to be more innovative and push the envelope a lot more. We are a far more robust team, a far more aggressive team. The environment is very dynamic. Everyone is buzzing with a lot of ideas and challenges, and our competitive spirit is very high.

Did you have to change anything about your managerial style?

The micromanagement has grown. The other thing I've had to change, in terms of keeping the team intact, has been to reach out to a lot more people from different parts of the country. So it definitely meant more Zoom calls. And it meant reaching out to people and giving my personal views, because there's been fear and insecurity due to the pandemic.

Mental health has also been a concern. And it was very, very important for us to keep the team motivated constantly. So I focused on keeping the teams a lot busier during this time. Which meant that I was giving them more tasks, newer things to do. But then a lot of it can't happen over emails. I think these things require meetings and the personal touch.

So the volume of work for me, in terms of micromanagement, increased. That personal touch was required to build faith within the organization. The company just had to tell employees that, you know, this is just a phase and we just need to slide through.

What collective goals do you set for your teams? What kinds of collective goals work and what collective goals don't work?

When you take risks, there are a lot of things that probably don't work. But then, at a larger, collective level, I always say don't take up anything if you don't believe in it. And you really have to be passionate about it. Also, in regard to the basic stuff, like the partnerships or any events that we do, we won't do something for the sake of doing it. Only if you believe in the idea, should you do it.

For instance, independent music. We truly feel the growth of independent music and the growth of independent artists in this country needs a mass-medium support like the radio. And we truly believe in the power of that music, because it is experimental music. It is fresh, and there's a lot of talent which is untapped. The only thing they're not getting is a platform. So as a philosophy, we believe in it. It's a passion project for the team that works on this project . . .

What doesn't work is individual work. But the moment there is a collective effort, we love to do that . . . The collective goals are these—we believe in inclusion, we believe in diversity, we believe in being passionate about things.

As a woman leader, how do you handle the men and women in your team? Do you use the same approach or do you change your style?

I think I am a taskmaster. I don't beat around the bush. So there are certain things which are for everyone, regardless of gender. That's my working style. Sometimes, I am probably tougher on the women, because they perform so much better. And I think they can do a lot better. I would never say that, you know, since I am a woman leader, and there are a lot of women on my team, I am softer on them. It's probably the opposite.

I feel that women bring in a lot of EQ [emotional quotient] to the working style. I believe you don't need to always show that you're very tough just because you're a woman leader. You don't smile, you won't crack jokes, you won't have any other interest, and you just project yourself as a really tough person. I don't think that is required. You can run a business with a certain empathy, being sensitive to working styles, to the teams, to the business itself and the environment. So I think women's quest to constantly prove themselves against men is the worst thing that can happen. What you need is to allow them to just better themselves. And that's where I am probably a little more tough. Yes, one always has to kind of be a little more flexible in style, especially for newcomers. But I truly don't think I differentiate . . .

What we've also done is to have more women in senior roles, and that has helped. It's not just about gender equality in workspaces; I think it's also extremely important to have more women leaders in senior positions. I think the environment is a lot more balanced. It's passionate. It's a lot more inclusive. And the men find it equally comforting to come and share their concerns as openly as any woman. I think that, too, means a lot, because it's not that ours is a women-driven organization. The men feel equally empowered. We need to create spaces where people have the freedom to come and speak their minds, speak their hearts, speak their thoughts. If you're able to do that, both for men and women, at an equal level, I think that's a good space to start.

Babita Baruah

Babita has been in advertising for twenty-five years and in one company, JWT, now called Wunderman Thompson. She has worked across the Kolkata, Mumbai and Delhi offices of Wunderman Thompson. She is currently the regional client lead for markets for WPP and before this she was managing partner, GTB India, working closely on the Ford business. She is a Chevening scholar and a speaker at the World Economic Forum and Harvard Business School. Babita is passionate about mentoring women.

In this interview she talks about building teams, handling people who flip their story in meetings, handling diversity and delivering on promises made to clients.

You are in the advertising/communications business. As an account director, you did not have any control over other functions in the agency, or over the brand managers on the client side. How do you work out

**a team in your mind when all of you are serving
the interests of the brand but come at it from vastly
different points of view?**

The role we play in the agency is both challenging and
exciting for this very reason. Exciting because as an agency,
we are considered stakeholders for the brand, and we play a
partnership role with clients. And challenging because there
are so many factors outside our control, despite our being
growth partners with the client. For that, we form a team with
a shared vision. A common purpose is vital for a team to come
together, stay together, stay motivated and work towards that
one goal. Once we have that alignment, different points of
view actually help bring in diverse perspectives. Because in
our industry, if we don't have diverse perspectives, we will
only have similar solutions for similar problems.

**I am sure you have come across many 'turncoats',
people who change their opinion after the boss has
spoken—whether it is in your team or the client's
team? How do you deal with such a person, and how
do you work with such a person after that?**

If you had asked me this question ten years ago, I would have
said that I would get angry, frustrated and that I would do
everything in my capacity to not work with the person. But
now, I try to approach this in two steps. First is to understand
the intent, and I've trained myself to separate the person from
the behaviour. I try to find out why the person changed his or

her opinion. For example, was it pressure from the boss? Was it the fear of losing the job? Now these are vulnerabilities. So once I understood the intent, my second step would always be to have an honest chat. It's definitely not easy when the turncoat is from the other side of the table. It's easier when it's a person you can have a conversation with easily. I don't start with, 'Why did you turn after you had agreed? You really let us down because you didn't stand up for us.' Instead, I try to understand why the person changed his or her mind. For example, today the conversation I would have would be like, 'I was really surprised when I heard your comment, because I thought we were aligned, but it doesn't matter. What made you change your mind? And is there anything we could have done? Because going forward, we have to work together, let's talk it out. I am sure we'll arrive at a solution.'

But there will be a small percentage of people who are very negative—so you can sometimes find that the turncoat is trying to really get you into trouble. Then there's no other way but to see how it pans out.

You have worked with people from different cultures in your career? Which cultures in your view produce naturally good team players and which cultures don't?

I have been lucky to have good team players across cultures. We are a process-driven organization, and it helps because the cultural differences are naturally smoothed out to a great extent. But the challenges we face are not so much culture-specific. It's not like I have this problem with a certain person because he or she is from a certain culture. It comes from a lack of understanding of cultural nuances, of cultural sensitivity. For example, a couple of years ago I was talking to someone, a non-Indian, about a campaign for a brand. And that person said, 'Just take a cricket bat and have a cricket field, and I am sure it's going to work in India.' The person was joking, but I took offence. We may be cricket-crazy, but please don't tell me that if you stick a cricket bat into the hand of a person and just show a game, it will make a brand in India. A nation is much more than that.

If you had to pick three cultures where you are least worried about work culture, commitment and good team players, which would those be?

It would have to be cultures from the Western world. I've always had the comfort of clarity of communication, very process-driven and very respectful of people's time. Very respectful of the weekends, respectful of the time spent with the family. For example, if a meeting runs over, it's not like you keep talking and you just don't even think it's important to apologize. Or if a meeting ends early, then say I am giving you some time so that you can spend it on yourself or with your family. These things matter.

The cultures I've had to struggle in my initial days with were one or two Asian markets. While working on a project there, I must admit, language was a problem. But it was also very difficult to gauge what the person wanted and whether they were responding to you. I have had challenges with non-confrontational cultures, where it is difficult to gauge alignment of views.

In your business, meeting deadlines is crucial. How do you align the team to deadline management? Does it often come at the cost of work–life balance?

It does. Anybody who wants a work–life balance should think before considering advertising. I think overall, the balance comes from the satisfaction one gets from work, because we are in the creative business. At the end, hours and hours of sleepless nights, fight and fatigue, when you see the work that has the ability to influence thinking, you feel it's worth it. And that's where I think the balance comes in.

We work on extremely tight deadlines at times. I sometimes feel that in our industry, we work better under pressure. I also feel deadlines are not a deterrent if the team is motivated. I am very motivated by that example of the janitor at NASA. When a visiting president asked the janitor what his job was, he said, 'Mr President, my job is to put a man on the moon.' Deadlines don't matter when you have a very motivated and charged team.

How do you manage your team in a business with long hours, clients rejecting the work and internal rejections? In all this, how do you keep the morale and motivation of your team up?

Our job has a lot of highs and a lot of lows. I'd be lying to myself if I say that everyone is highly motivated at all times.

It is demotivating when an idea is rejected; also, a lot depends on the way it is rejected. Sometimes there's no reason given for the rejection, except, 'I don't like it. Show me something else.'

This is where the leader can make a difference. I always feel the leader has to be at the receiving end of the dartboard, and also be a bouncing board and a springboard for ideas. Make the team define for themselves why they have chosen this profession. What gives them joy? What are the hurdles? I personally feel we have to be very generous when we compliment people and really recognize people for the work they do. We must say, 'Hey, the idea may not have gone through, but I know the nights and the days that you have worked and thank you for that.' I think gratitude and celebration, having people's back, really revive the morale to a great extent. And even if people go through that, they bounce back very quickly.

Your business has a bunch of stars. How do you manage their egos without upsetting the team?

Egos are part of the world itself, especially when it comes to successful people. Our industry is no different. And people who are impacted by it the most are usually younger team members. They find it very stressful to work with people with egos, stars and senior people. But the younger team members must understand why people are stars in the first place. They are stars because they bring in name, fame and business to the organization. Because of that, we are all proud of them as an organization.

I think the role of a leader is to talk to people who are successful. Because you are at a senior level, you can have a heart-to-heart conversation. I have always had very honest conversations, saying, 'Maybe you don't intend to or maybe you don't even notice it, but those kids, or that team or that person, finds it so hard to even walk up to you.' And usually the conversation goes down well because you have dissipated the tension. You have to intervene in this casual manner because, remember, you're dealing with egos. Egos cannot be dealt with through egotism. So if I start writing formal emails, or walk into the conference room and say, 'You know, the agenda for today is the way you behave with my team', believe me, there will be no going back after that.

It's a mix of egos, talent, conversation, fun, debates, crying in the washroom and fights that makes up our industry and some of our best ideas. We just have to embrace all of it.

Creative people are often known to be unruly, irreverent and difficult to manage. How do you bring a sense of discipline in a team where people thrive on creativity and rule-breaking?

Discipline as a term itself doesn't go very well with our industry, especially with creativity. Creativity is like water, it is free-flowing. And if you channelize it too much, you don't get the magic of that waterfall or, you know, the music of the stream. So discipline, or too much of it, may actually become a straightjacket for free-flowing thought.

Earlier, I would look at discipline in the strict sense of the word. For example, if somebody didn't reach office by nine thirty, I would ask what time the person had left office. Today, I realize that we do have flexibility of working time, which means you can walk in an hour or so late because you had worked late, and I understand that some people work late because they work better towards the end of the day. The flexibility of a few hours doesn't mean everybody can walk in whenever they want—it means you can relax the timing a little. This automatically makes everybody comfortable.

I feel if a leader and the team have great trust between each other, with that trust comes accountability. Then you don't need these other forms of discipline, which we somehow feel are very important. Honestly, discipline is only important if it is leading to greater productivity. If it leads people to feel dejected, I would never encourage that kind of discipline.

You have stayed with Wunderman Thompson for close to twenty-five years, in an era when a lot of people like to climb the ladder with lateral movements while changing jobs. What worked for you?

I think I love my organization too much. But having said that, I have had lateral moves within the organization. I have worked on almost every category. I have worked across three cities and three offices. While being within the organization, I have always found ways, or the organization has found ways, to bring in that variety so that I've never felt like I am stuck in one place.

I feel, however, that times have changed today. I actually encourage young people to be more open to exploration. Because the choices are much more than what we had earlier. Youngsters today—the millennials, and now we will have the first of Generation Z also getting into the workforce—come from a very different world. There are so many options out there for them that I feel this whole concept that was drilled into us by our parents—the words 'stability', 'consistency', sticking to one place—I don't think it's relevant any more.

Gautam Khanna

Gautam is a graduate of IIT Kanpur and IIM Calcutta. He has over thirty years of experience. He was executive director and country business lead of 3M for India and Sri Lanka. He is currently the CEO of P.D. Hinduja Hospital in Mumbai.

In 2021, Gautam was awarded the title of one of India's best leaders in times of crisis by Great Place to Work. His handling of the COVID crisis and the multiple demands made on him during the pandemic were a lesson in patience and leadership.

In this interview he talks about managing the COVID situation, how a leader aligns people and energizes them, and what leaders should stand for.

You head one of the most premium hospital chains in the country. How did you prepare your team to face a digital world in the pandemic, and what new practices have you adopted as a team?

Like everyone else, we were thrown off by the suddenness of the whole thing. We got the first case of COVID in our hospital on 12 March 2020. Just a week before, we had decided we wouldn't admit any COVID patients in the normal patient area and would ask patients to declare their travel history, etc. But a patient made a false declaration, that he had not travelled to Dubai, and got himself admitted to our ICU. The same afternoon we were discussing what infrastructure changes we might need just in case we got a COVID patient. And in the evening we came to know that we already had a patient. Frankly, I was concerned. We had to immediately quarantine eighty-nine hospital staff who had come in contact with the patient. The government inspectors wanted us to close down the hospital in the night itself to prevent spread to other patients. Hence, our priority in the evening was to safely transfer the patient to an approved government hospital and prevent the hospital from closing down.

We knew we had to act fast, but I realized that my team and I didn't know what to do because it was an unprecedented situation. But because you are the CEO, you have to make decisions and guide your teams. The next day we decided to set up a COVID area and called for a meeting with many staff members across hierarchies. We were a very hierarchy-conscious hospital. But I encouraged all of them to sit together and resolve all the issues. Within a week, the junior people were getting empowered and making decisions.

A major problem we faced was in figuring out proper clinical protocols because nobody had ever done this before. I told my team to do research, gather knowledge and bring it up for discussion. They quickly came back with suggestions, and we implemented some of those protocols. One thing I learnt from this episode is that saying 'I am ignorant, and I can't do the job' does not work now in the digital world. You have all kinds of information available easily. You just need to be willing to learn. So the team was asked to get ready with all information possible.

To streamline the decision-making process, I divided the meetings into two sections: clinical and non-clinical. I involved everyone and told them openly: 'If I close it, this is the impact we'll have. Paying salaries will be an issue. But if I don't close it, this is what will happen. What do you suggest?' Now, it didn't become my decision alone; it was their collective decision. This empowerment really helped them take quick action. To ensure social distancing, we implemented multiple shifts and a new rota was prepared, and we created these small groups empowered to make decisions. We also closed down the OPD to prevent crowding. That meant we were losing business. Hence, the team switched to digital platforms so that patients who could not visit the hospital and were scared of coming could consult with the doctors without any difficulties. Apart from that, we made sure, through regular communication via email, that every employee was kept in the loop about what was going on and what steps we were taking.

As the time progressed, people's roles and responsibilities were being changed, and young people were handling new responsibilities. I also told my senior staff on calls that we would not speak in the first half of the meeting—we would only listen. It's a very small thing to say, but look at it from the junior employees' point of view. They see that the seniors are listening, so they are open to giving you information about what is happening in the hospital. That way we were able to make better decisions. If the seniors had started telling them what to do, the juniors would have depended on their instructions alone.

There were also fears among the staff that they might lose their jobs if any of their decisions backfired. So, I told them, 'You are free to make mistakes as long as you are doing it for the best interests of the patient and the hospital. If there is a problem, say the CEO told me to do it. I will take responsibility even if it is about a decision I am not aware of.' That gave them confidence to keep making quick decisions, which was the need of the hour.

The twist in the tale came in the early days of the pandemic when, on my doctors' advice, I stopped going to the hospital because of some clinical conditions. About a month later, I found out that some people were saying they would not come to work if the CEO wasn't coming to the hospital. I had to go against my doctors' recommendations to ensure employee morale and motivation. Since then I have been coming to the office every day to give my staff the confidence and serve the patients.

The health business is a trust business. What do you do as a leader to instil in your team behaviours that build trust?

Small things. For example, in our hospital, nobody is allowed to take a tip. Patients need to know that you are not working for money, so they start trusting the staff. In every communication meeting, I would tell my staff that your loyalties should not lie with an individual; your loyalties should lie with the organization and the patient. Right at the beginning of the COVID-19 outbreak, I told everyone: 'In a crisis, it is very, very easy to lose integrity. Do not compromise on integrity and ethics.' I issued a warning that if anyone was found guilty of flouting rules, they would lose their job.

I use positive reinforcement in order to inculcate a sense of dedication in my staff. In one of the meetings, I got to know that we had dealt with nearly 1 crore patients in the past 10–20 years. I told them, 'Even if there are four people per family, you are now getting the blessings of 4 crore people! If the patients don't come back to you, you don't have a job, you don't have the means to take care of your family. Treat the patients the way you would treat your family members.' Also, through my rounds, I keep an open communication line with my staff and patients. That gives them the confidence that if they have any problem, there's someone right at the top who will listen to it and fix it. In my experience, this is an effective way to stop the rise of any kind of trust deficit.

I also believe that empowering your team is a great way to build trust. For that, I encourage my team to empower their respective teams. I ask them to become as approachable to their team members as I am to them. I tell them: 'If I treat you as an equal, why would you treat your juniors as unequals? I trust you, so you should trust them. If I take care of your mistakes, you should take care of those of your teams.'

Additionally, there are a lot of systems in place, checks and balances to see that nobody is misusing the system. For example, we regularly check if diagnostic tests are unnecessarily prescribed or a surgery classification is being changed just to charge more money. In that case, we would ask the person concerned the rationale behind those decisions. So they know that their activities are being monitored, and we do not want to drop the checks at any stage. In short, we have a robust system and processes in place to ensure nobody misuses their powers. That goes a long way in building trust between the hospital and the patient.

How has the business of health care changed after the pandemic, and how did you communicate this to your team? What development initiatives are needed in a post-pandemic world with respect to health-care teams?

When the pandemic hit us, the main thing was to maintain business continuity, which was not possible without some fundamental changes. For example, in April 2020, we were thinking of starting tele-consult because everybody was doing it, but the idea didn't click easily, because it's not easy for organizations like ours to do anything new in a short time. But on my insistence, we started consultations on WhatsApp calls and gradually moved to a software where patients could upload reports and download prescriptions. I told my team to be aware of the consequences of not changing with time. I put forward some facts before them and told them that running a hospital would be difficult if everyone insisted on doing things the old way. They understood my point and adapted to the change.

Development initiatives in the health-care industry could be looked at from the innovation point of view. With technology on our side, our teams became innovative. So, we designed a medical package for people who were home-quarantined for fourteen days. Over those fourteen days, we would take care of the patients, our doctor would give consultations four times, our nurse would monitor vitals every eight hours, our counsellor would tell you the diet, there was a psychiatrist who would do your psychological counselling. It also worked for people who did not want to visit the hospital.

How do teams in MNCs work differently from teams in Indian organizations?

The big difference is on accountability and performance management. In MNCs, you are accountable, and you will be asked to leave if the performance is not up to the mark. In Indian companies, the relationships and loyalties are often quite important, even if the performance is not good. So that is a big difference. And that determines the culture of the place—what you would have taken three days to do in an MNC would take three months to do here. The second thing is the retirement age. In an MNC, you would retire at sixty or fifty-eight or whatever is the number. But in Indian companies you could last beyond the retirement age. This practice of granting extensions changes the culture of the company—young and ambitious people become disinclined to join the organization, because they know there is little or no room to grow as these senior fellows will never leave. As a result, you don't get the right kind of talent. So the big difference between MNCs and Indian companies has to do with the kind of talent they are able to employ and attract.

The other thing is about systems. MNCs have very strong systems and processes in place to minimize the scope for arbitrary decisions. Sometimes MNCs may be bureaucratic, but they have systems to control their people and ensure nobody deviates from the rulebook. But if you are an Indian company, you may not have systems as strong as an MNC, and there is always room for individual decisions.

What's the difference between the way teams in product organizations and teams in service organizations work? Which measures are common, and which different, when it comes to team effectiveness?

In a product company, the first thing is that you may have some time to fix things, because the product-selling cycle could be a month or a week. In services, on the other hand, if you don't do it now, you've lost an opportunity.

In the services industry, teamwork is more important. In case of hospitals, for example, the overall experience of a patient is not dependent on one person or department; it is dependent on all the people in the chain—be it the security personnel, the lift operator, the housekeeping fellows, nurses, doctors or the billing guys. Everybody has to work in sync in a services company to ensure a pleasant experience for the customer. In a product company, on the other hand, even if they don't work in sync, it's okay, you can manage. In a product company you can have a star salesman who doesn't get along with anyone, and it will still work. But in a services organization, you can't do that. Because a patient can get infuriated because of even one weak link. Therefore, working in sync is of the utmost importance in a services organization like ours.

Anusha Suryanarayan

Anusha is an HR professional and is currently the CHRO of Signify India. She was earlier the Nokia India HR director. Anusha has extensive experience across HR business partnering, talent management, organizational design and development learning.

In this interview she talks about working in a matrix, leading teams and challenges in managing people, and provides clarity on how to be an effective team leader.

In any team, what's the role of a leader, and what's the role of a fellow colleague in building good team spirit?

I think both are important. If nobody follows you, you're not a leader. A leader needs followers probably as much as a follower needs to look up to a leader. A follower is somebody who actually has a lot of influence, and who can make you literally from zero to hero. Because it's all about how many followers you have today . . . Anybody can be a leader. You

167

don't need to have a team below you to be a leader. I know enough people who are individual contributors and exert such great influence around them that they are leaders in every way.

So I think in today's context, the whole leader and follower idea is really about the kind of influence you exert. And this, I think, started changing quite some time back, as more and more organizations became matrix organizations. In a matrix world, you could have multiple people to report to, and you could have a team that gets created, disbanded, created, disbanded. It is not about the hierarchy and how many people you have under you. And in the digital and social-media world, honestly, I think a lot of it has come into question again. But here again, it's about longevity. How often can you create an impact as an influencer in the organization? It's the organization first, then it's the team, and then it's you. A true leader will always think this way. It's never me first. And that really makes the leader stand out. These traits are not built one fine day when you get into a senior position. These are things that you start developing as you grow in the organization. A lot of it is about attitude and mindset.

Do people who report to those in leadership positions play any role in making them leaders?

If you don't have followers, can you still call yourself a leader? In today's world, reporting is not that big of a deal. You could have one person reporting or twenty. What matters is how you are able to influence people, how you connect the strategy to their work, to show them a larger vision that unites them, to bring them together, to help them understand why they matter, to stay connected through communication. And to be able to help them grow and develop. One leader that I know used to say, 'My only job is to make myself redundant.' Which basically meant that he was grooming people under him to take over from him. And that comes from a very strong leadership stance, because you have to be that confident and secure. And also that level of trust has to exist between the team and the leader.

What signs do you look for in a good team in business? And what variables define a good team?

I think the first thing that unites a team is a common purpose. So you may have a very diverse team with a very diverse set of skills, but as long as the starting point is a unified goal and vision that you all are pushing towards, that helps the team come together. And I don't think there is any such thing as a good team. Any team can be good, depending on the purpose they've been put together for and the environment they are given to operate in. So a fantastic football team may play cricket very badly. It's all about a common unified purpose and why the team has come together.

The second thing is having very clear roles. In this day and age, you have multiple overlaps between KPIs. A salesperson's goal may be completely eating into a supply chain person's KPI directly. You all have your individual goals that you need to manage. How are all of these coming together to do the right thing for the organization? What's the organization looking to achieve? So you need to have some boundaries in terms of what everybody is contributing to the overall team.

The third thing is agility. It has to be an agile team. And when I say agile, it's about how quickly the team members can sense changes in the environment and how they can mould themselves to move quickly in a different direction.

The last is communication. You can never communicate enough. Ensuring that you're connected, in today's virtual world, is very critical. I think these are some of the things that help make a team good. The team is as good as the purpose it sets out to achieve.

In business, what are the signals that you might be working with a poor team? What do you do when you have a poor team as an HR leader in an organization?

There are many red flags. The first one is about the breakdown of communication and trust. That's usually what starts coming through when you indicate that something is not right or when you have people leaving. And now, HR folks have multiple metrics that they use. I think the most common one is the engagement survey. These days, people have these quarterly pulse checks and surveys, where on a quarterly basis you can check the NPS (net promoter score) of a team in terms of how engaged it is or it isn't.

There are various ways to check team engagement. The biggest one is through asking: Would you recommend somebody else from outside to come and join this team? If the answer is no, then something's not right. Organizations have different ways to measure engagement. You know, they'll do pulse checks. And of course, there are lagging indicators, like attrition. So you look at how many people have left a team and at anything else that comes across as dysfunctional. The best way to pick that up is through team dialogues. The other thing that we do, especially when there is a new leader in a team, is something called manager assimilation. Three months down the line, when the team and the leader have had a chance to understand each other, we do a session between the two. If things are going well, then great. If not, we look at the areas we need to work on.

You have seen team behaviour in great times and the same team behaving badly in times of poor results. What would you infer from it?

It depends on a lot of external factors. A lot of it has to do with how agile that team is. So in this day and age, you have to be on your toes; you can't do the same things you did yesterday. For instance, the team of people that came together to figure out what the organization needed to do in the first wave of COVID had to do drastically different things in wave two. The COVID response team was what we called it; it was looking at very different problems in the first wave. And if we had done the same things this time around, it would have not worked. We had to do very different things, because the second wave demanded something very different. So you need to understand and gauge situation, and then be agile enough to change the way you work and change what you're doing to meet the new requirements.

Why do well-performing teams fail sometimes? Is it skill mismatch or just the timing?

A well-performing team also needs to reinvent itself to meet the new challenge. It's as simple as that. Now, that could mean multiple things. It could mean skill set changes. It could mean your purpose has changed and you're still working towards the old purpose. It could mean that there are certain people who are demotivated and that's not being taken care of or managed the way it should be. There is no one factor that makes a particular team successful in one go and not in the other. It depends on the situation. At the end of the day, a team needs to rethink everything that it does to meet a new challenge. Don't approach a new challenge the same way because even if the challenge looks the same, there may be ten things about it that are not the same any more.

Who is responsible for team learning? The leader, HR? The team members? What stops teams from learning collectively?

Learning is everybody's responsibility. Everybody is individually in charge of their learning. And all the more so because a lot of the platforms that have been used, especially in the past year, are digital in nature. So on Netflix or Facebook, the content that you consume is not what somebody else wants you to see or is expecting you to consume. It's about what piques your interest, and you go there and pick and choose what you want. That's learning these days. It is no more about sitting in a classroom for eight hours. It's all about virtual and digital learning. Sharing an example of my own organization, we have a fantastic global platform which allows you to choose what you want to learn.

How does one handle a matrix team as opposed to a direct-relationship team?

The matrix is here to stay. We often complain about so many meetings. But the only reason that these meetings happen is because there are so many core dependencies, which you've got to work with in a collaborative manner to make something happen. Also, it's a very thinly manned and a de-layered workforce. So in all these scenarios, matrix has become the way of working.

In HR, you have HR business partners, and then you have talent acquisition, or you have centres of excellence. Now, in many matrix structures, the HR business partners report directly to the CHRO. But the centres of excellence report directly outside. Does that mean that I have only business partners reporting to me and have no control over the talent acquisition team, because the talent acquisition head doesn't report to me? No, that's not the way it works. It doesn't matter where your reporting line goes. What matters are the stakeholders. The stakeholders become critical here, and not just your immediate manager but all the people that you work with. Your systems need to support a matrix way of working. And of course, culturally, you need to be able to support that.

How does a leader handle a matrix team and a direct-reporting team?

I think it's about influencing. It's about what you're trying to drive. If what I am trying to achieve involves ten people, eight of whom don't report to me, but all of us are working towards this goal, then I will find a way to get this team together. In many cases, though, it does require some amount of learning. It's not always easy to just do that. But I do think that the cultural set-up of the organization makes a difference. In a very flat kind of structure and a place where every headcount is critical, the work that you do will end up having core dependencies in such a manner that you will have to pull a team of people together, many of whom may not report to you. Many times I have to work with finance business partners, or I have to ensure that I am pulling people in from marketing or PR or digital marketing teams, because a lot of the work that I do also sits in these buckets. Now, they can react in two ways. They can say, I do marketing and don't have anything to do with HR. Or they can understand what the problem is and make sure that they help solve it.

How have you seen team behaviour and culture change from the pre-pandemic to post-pandemic world?

It seems like it's a new world. It's like we've all left this one planet and have gone to another, where we only see each other on screens. A lot of time and effort in the first wave just went in helping people adapt to this new way of working, building their virtual connections and helping them in other ways. To ensure business continuity, you have to ensure your teams are engaged and motivated. This was a huge challenge, and everything was shut.

We discovered many ways in which you can go digital. I think our digital footprint exploded. We found all kinds of ways to create this engagement. So we actually realized that you can bring families into some of these engagement sessions, more so than we could earlier. We had yoga sessions in the mornings, where we had the spouses join in. And we did this for our customers as well. We had drawing competitions for kids. We had an annual event called the CEO Awards for three hours. And the people who won the awards were applauded, because they had their families sitting around when this was going on. The kind of response we got after this was fantastic.

But this didn't happen automatically. It took us months of struggling to see what we could do to really stay connected as an organization. We had open sessions where we asked team leaders to hold little coffee corners—we call them virtual cafés—where employees actually came into the sessions and talked about how they were dealing with stuff at home, kids, work, etc. We also had mental health experts hold sessions. During the second wave, we had a lot of sessions around how to handle grief and how to deal with personal loss. I think COVID has just forever changed the way we work, connect and operate.

Devendra Chawla

Devendra Chawla is a multifaceted, eloquent leader. He worked in Coca-Cola (Route to Market), was the CEO of Future Consumer Ltd and the COO of Walmart. He is currently MD and CEO of Spencer's Retail and Nature's Basket. He is an authority on retail formats and marketing, and has been awarded many times in his illustrious career.

DC is a sough-after speaker and has done many sessions for CII, FICCI, AMCHAM and AIMA. He is also a board member and mentor to many start-ups.

You have worked both in MNCs and Indian organizations. How does the concept of a team and teamwork vary between the two? What are the subtleties that one must understand?

You need to study this from the perspective of India's own economic growth trajectory and its ability to provide an atmosphere conducive to the birth of successful, process-driven as well as entrepreneurial companies. As we have our own FAANGs and companies servicing global consumers, the line that once separated MNCs from the Indian ones, in terms of quality, will keep getting blurred day by day.

Having said that, a team is a team, and its basic tenets remain the same. The concept of teamwork depends not only on the organization but also on the culture of the society in which the business is operating. Therefore, I would not want to differentiate on the basis of whether it is an MNC or an Indian company. If you're a couple-of-billion-dollar organization in India, then your structure, hierarchy, matrix, etc., is much like an MNC's.

I started my career with Asian Paints, and I can't think of a more professional organization. I think this conversation about 'difference between an Indian company and an MNC' is no longer relevant. It was, when MNCs started coming up, in the '80s and '90s, and there was some fascination to work for them. It augmented your social status then. Not any more. Why would the biggest Indian ecommerce website be any less than an American one operating in India?

People these days want to work for a winning culture. Take the food-delivery platforms in India. Where are the MNCs there? There was one which was part of a ride-hailing company. But that one lost the war and is no longer in the game, and the Indian ones in that segment are making waves. So, as far as I am concerned, I will work for a company which has a winning culture. This coming generation is least bothered about the Indian vs MNC debate. They talk about stuff like ESG, women's participation, LGBTQ policy, environment, sustainability process, etc. And this isn't just lip service; they really believe in it. My daughter, for example, says she will work for a company which holds better ESG standards. She wouldn't care if it's an Indian company or an MNC.

There is another side to this debate. Earlier, MNCs could build businesses because they had SOPs, processes, procedures. But Indian companies have very well caught up with MNCs with regard to SOPs, processes, work culture, employee benefits, recourse to complaints and whistle-blower policy.

How should one work in a matrix team as opposed to in a normal-hierarchy team?

In a layered-hierarchy structure, you have to align yourself with one person who will appraise you, judge you and decide your career. In a matrix culture, people work in teams, or loosely assigned teams, on projects. So, it all depends on what culture you are trying to build. In a start-up, for example, there are so many things which need to be worked upon and discussed. Discoveries and learnings need to be shared. A matrix structure fits them.

From an associate point of view, it means aligning yourself to a larger objective, where the objective is divided among more than one person. You are talking to two or three different people at a time. It means that you give importance to a dual reporting system, because you inherently believe that each boss can add a different value or each function or role above you will add a different value for you to succeed in your role. At the same time, you cannot ignore its flip side: while the matrix structure allows associates to communicate across departments and associates can enhance skills by taking part in various projects, it can also lead to challenges as authority conflicts may creep in between project and functional managers. This can add to the confusion and may even cause conflict, especially where both managers have equal authority.

What is the difference between managing functional teams and execution teams as a leader, or between head office teams and field teams?

One key difference is that while the goals need to be extremely clear and numerically quantifiable for all teams, they are a bit more important for the execution team. Apart from that, there need to be clear deadlines, and the team effort needs to be measured. Also, you need to get a buy-in so that the teams on the ground believe in the plan, and if you manage an execution team, celebrate their wins more often.

Another major difference between managing a head office or corporate team, and a field team or an execution team, is that the field team is more focused on the 'here and now', the short-term goals. On the other hand, the primary focus of the corporate team is to provide support. Also, more often than not, corporate teams have to work in a cross-functional set-up where they depend on other departments to get their work done. But in an execution team, it is a straight line down.

For example, a sales rep won't have three bosses; he'll have one called sales supervisor. And a sales supervisor has a boss called area sales manager. If you're a worker in the factory, your supervisor is the only boss. Period. You don't have many other bosses to report to. So as you go down the execution matrix, it's a more direct line of reporting, and it's more here and now, more short-term, more defined, more numbers, where you can do a yes or no binary, whether the target was achieved or not.

As far as managing the two teams is concerned, field teams are more entrepreneurial, relentless, energetic and target-driven. If I go and tell somebody, *sale le ke aana hai* [make the sale], he may think of new ideas to do that. They're very driven by numbers, they're go-getters, and sometimes they're impatient to get things done. So the way to lead them is different. But when it comes to your corporate, HO teams, they are functional experts; they tend to think analytically; they have more systems and are process-driven.

Who is responsible for team development? The team leader, HR or the team members themselves?

Good leaders add value to their direct reports and teams, and they don't delegate only to HR. Instead, they allow the HR to supplement. The success of a team depends on the strategies formed and the leadership given by the team leader, who is your immediate supervisor. And he or she is supposed to identify which stage the team is at and provide adequate support for the team's progress. Like in our case, in a store, it's the store manager or the team leader who will make the difference for that day.

Now, whose job is it to develop a team? I think every supervisor has to take ownership for their direct reports, development, and it will go on right till the CEO. The HR has to do it for the whole company, as a function; it is their job to provide gap assessment and training, and to equip people with more learning and more skill sets.

I also think there's a lack of one-on-ones between people, for a conversation on the development of people. The idea of leadership has become more like a person addressing an army of people or giving a lecture, but I think a lot of one-on-one interactions need to be done at every level. If you're a VP, with three or five GMs reporting to you, you have to spend time with them one on one, understand them and work with the HR. If not the HR, work with them directly, support them, give them projects where you feel they will be able to learn about that skill set, fix that gap. So, every manager or supervisor has to develop their teams. It will be a disservice to only do your targets or numbers or objectives at hand, and not groom them for the future. HR won't know about an individual's skill sets or lack thereof. It's not possible. HR may arrange for a common learning opportunity for all, but within that everybody is not equal. Some may need more, some may need less. And who knows that? The team leader. So, the team leader will do a disservice if he only keeps working and keeps meeting company targets. He has to also take ownership of team development.

How did you manage the team through the pandemic? Any tips for team leaders?

The pandemic separated the wheat from the chaff. Not only did it redefine many rules, it also turned a whole new leaf as far as leadership lessons were concerned. No MBA or books taught us how to go through a pandemic. First of all, you acknowledge that it is a different world, and you do not try to become a superwoman or superman. And you lead in a crisis by serving. So, leadership in the pandemic was at the lowest level.

Because we sell essentials, our stores were open every day during the lockdown, and thousands of my people were working continually. People understand that they are required to serve society at this time. You respect and honour them, and make them realize they are no less than a health-care worker in terms of importance because they deliver essentials. In such a situation, as the CEO, you prioritize taking care of your people, ensuring they are safe, making them aware that what they're doing is larger than just a job for salary. I think if you do that, that's enough.

The pandemic also showed there is so much goodness in people. When the lockdown was imposed, more staff turned up to work than we expected, even though public transport had nearly come to a standstill. Some walked several kilometres to reach the stores. It was so touching. And that's when you're forced to see that leadership is not about command and control. You didn't have to become their boss in the pandemic. You had to serve them. My questions to them used to be: What can I do for you? What do you need? What can I get you for safety? Can I get you a car to pick you up? How can I make your life easier? Because you're serving a bigger cause, I can only support you. It's called servant leadership. If I serve my team, they will serve the customer. That's the only way to work. I never had to tell anyone to come to work. In the corporate world, it is taught that you have to guide people. So every boss's job is to direct people as to what is to be done. The pandemic changed all these notions.

We were the world's first company that tied up with Uber, Rapido and Swiggy to make sure essentials were delivered to people who could not step out. When you start delivering positive things for society, that team gets charged and feels aligned to the purpose and feel that not only are we able to serve society, but we are also winning. I learnt in this pandemic that leadership is not at the top, it's at the bottom. I can't force people to go out every day and make forty deliveries at people's homes and take the risk of COVID. If they don't want to do it on their own, nobody can force them to do it. But they wanted to do it, they felt a sense of purpose. And they did it. That's how I managed my team. The pandemic has shown that there are many ways to be a leader. If you have a sense of purpose and truly believe in serving the consumer, then I think you're a leader.

We tied up with hospitals and increased insurance for our people. We took care of people who went to the hospital. We vaccinated all staff at the company's cost. The least I can do is take care of our own people. You build a culture of care. You build a culture of serving, and you build a culture of servant leadership.

In a social media/connected world, teams don't like it if outsiders talk directly to you, the boss, about issues they face with your organization. How do you handle this?

Social media is making customer service more efficient by calling it out. It is a great feedback tool, and brands have to stay ahead and use this to the companies' advantage by solving issues fast, so that you are able to convert it into advocacy. But first, companies require a certain kind of open-mindedness to accept this new channel of receiving feedback. Not embracing it will be at the organization's own peril.

As a boss, I think it's very important to hear people out. So, if somebody wants to reach out to you, and wants to talk to you, has a grievance or has feedback, you have to help them out.

If the team doesn't like outsiders reaching out to me directly, I can't do anything about it. I think the days of heartburn are over, because today, if there's any problem in anything, people directly reach out to me all the time through social media. Not just vendors, even customers. That's what social media has done. So managers who've grown up in the past era of command and control and hierarchy, and information control, are going to have a hard time. Today, they have no control, and it is a good loss of control. You have to be accountable to society, to vendors, to customers. And if you're not taking care of them, if they have a grievance, then today, thanks to social media, they will directly reach the boss or whoever they want. So people who don't like it have to learn to deal with it. Because this is the new reality. You have to be efficient, and you have to serve the customer. Otherwise, your lacunas will be brought to the attention of the hierarchy in ways you can't even imagine.

Managing Your Team: Points for Reflection

1. The idea of leading a team is not to be the same with everyone. One needs to be fair as a team leader but treat each team member differently based on their needs.
2. A good team is a combination of a good leader, good colleagues and commitment to the team cause. Good team leaders do not play one against the other; they urge the team to a new high.
3. Insecure and incompetent team leaders are the worst thing for a good team. This type of leader ends up destroying the team.
4. A team leader's energy will get sucked up by colleagues—the prima donnas at one end and people lacking in will at the other end. Both drain your energy in different ways.
5. The most valuable resource a leader can give a team is his/her time. Make your time available and make it count.

Section III

Managing Your Business

Morris Tabaksblat, ex-CEO, Unilever, was addressing potential general managers at the Four Acres training centre in London many years ago. One of the participants asked him what he considered was the toughest part of his job as chairman. Morris thought for a while and said, 'Dealing with twenty-five- to thirty-year-old young analyst investors. If I say we have grown top line but not delivered profit, they ask me if this strategy is sustainable. If I say I've grown profit but sacrificed top line, they asked me if this is sensible. If I say I protected share, then they ask me if share is the be-all and end-all of a business. It's a no-win situation, whatever you say.'

That exchange and challenge is from a few years ago. It's even more difficult today as the number of variables to judge a business have multiplied and the scrutiny, whether you are a listed entity or an unlisted one, is just as intense.

Unilever is at a trough with a rejected bid for Glaxo Consumer products and a reorganization from a matrix structure to a category structure. I am not sure if they are addressing the correct problem since they have not performed for the last five years compared to peer companies. Structure change is 'recipe 101' in the CEO answer book, when in essence structure should follow strategy. A structure change shows that action has been taken, and it buys the CEO 12–18 months' time.

There are 230 million businesses in the world, there are 70,000 to 80,000 MNCs globally, and there are 2.1 million companies in India and 63 million MSMEs. Every business, big or small, must be run well. Every big business of today was once a small business. Let's look at the five fundamentals P's when you run a business. These will always matter, and the context will add newer focus areas. The Five P's are:

 i. Position in industry you operate in
 ii. Profitability of your business
 iii. Process discipline in the organization
 iv. People
 v. Public image

Position

The first is relative position. This is the position you hold in the industry and the eco system. Do you matter? Some people will argue that they are not able to define the industry. So if you want a simple definition, ask two questions: Who wins when you lose? And who loses when you win? The sum total of the two is the rough arena where you are playing. A good example of what I am saying is what we could term 'impulse'. Look at all the categories at a cash counter anywhere in the world. There will be chocolates, cigarettes, confectionery, soft drinks, chips, etc. All of them are fighting for the customer's wallet at the cash counter, even though cigarettes and chocolates look like chalk and cheese.

In looking at an industry, analysts typically tend to look at volume, value and profit leadership. I would add a fourth element, which is thought leadership. Very rarely does a brand or company have all four. Google and Colgate are two rare examples.

The old school of thought favoured share. Over time, as technology and capabilities became available freely across the board and media vehicles got fragmented, all market leaders came under stress, and we saw many profitable niches spring up. The digital world has made this trend an avalanche. In every sector, from food and personal care to wellness, unmentionables, etc., the digital direct-to-consumer brands have grown fast and at a premium to the industry leaders.

Consumer companies have market share as a good measure of competitiveness. In B2B businesses, there is no market share data available and hence many B2B industries tend to look at capacity share and then look at capacity utilization as a surrogate, assuming they have sold what they produced. This has two flaws. First, what's sold is, in many cases, channel-stuffing in categories like cement, paint, apparel, etc. So if one doesn't know the true offtake, one can get misled by primary sales. Second, in B2B businesses the price varies between key customers. So profit pools are not readily available to analysts. Analysts tend to have trade conversations or expert conversations to triangulate sales, inventory and price.

This market share thought is very important. It led Ajit Haksar at ITC to set up a special market share panel with the

IMRB in the 1960s, and it led Hindustan Unilever to establish the Household Buying panel in the 1970s. I don't see leaders of any industry today chasing this measure with the same zeal.

If your brand or company is the brand leader or leader in a sales geography or channel, then the only success measure is to increase the lead over the next competitor. When Nokia became market leader after overtaking Motorola, the only theme that resonated across Nokia sales and marketing teams was 'extend the lead'.

If your brand or sales geography or company or channel is No. 2, then the only question you must answer to grow your business is, 'How do I narrow the lead vs No. 1?'

The No. 3 brand in most categories across the board does not have a market share of more than 10 per cent. So, if you are outside the top three, then the question to manage your business is, 'How do I break into the top three?' This sounds easy but is difficult in most cases. It's difficult because market leaders are not sitting idle, and if you have to grow faster than the market, then you have to invest and take a hit on profitability. There are no free lunches in business. The chances of sustaining price-led share gains in today's marketplace are slim, even if you are a tech or digital company. All digital companies have put in enormous capital and effort in customer acquisition costs. The moment the offer is not attractive, the consumer shifts. In the analysis I have done or seen, the entry of a digital brand into every sector down-trades the profitability of the sector as value migrates downwards, and over time, after the initial value destruction, the industry or segment profit pool starts to grow.

Price-cutting or schemes to trade or high consumer acquisition costs are never sustainable. Every business leader plays with these because he/she convinces the management or board or the parent company that the cost of doing nothing is even more dangerous. In all my years of sitting on boards and review committees, I have never heard a CEO say that the competition is sensible and is not playing the price game. Never! So, the strategy of running a business seems to be more competition-focused and less of any other advantage variable.

Innovation was a way of disrupting a market, getting a higher premium and building some trust. However, we are seeing a lot of innovation being given away at less than the cost to the consumer or ecosystem.

Organizations That Failed to Change and Organizations That Changed with Success

Failed to Change	Changed with Success
KODAK	PAYPAL
NOKIA	GOOGLE
XEROX	FACEBOOK
BLOCKBUSTER	APPLE
YAHOO	NETFLIX
BLACKBERRY	AMAZON
MYSPACE	SPOTIFY
POLAROID	AMERICAN EXPRESS
MOTOROLA	WIPRO
COMPAQ	
AMERICA ONLINE	
NORTEL	

Source: https://www.chargify.com/blog/6-companies-that-succeeded-by-changing-their-business-model; https://www.valuer.ai/blog/50-examples-of-corporations-that-failed-to-innovate-and-missed-their-chance

The three innovations I have seen spring up as the digital model takes shape are: business model innovation, packaging innovation and concept innovation.

If you want to lead a business tomorrow, you need to be an agile structural thinker. You need the ability to see trends, assess what they mean quickly and constantly evolve the strategy to seek a better business position. MNCs are unlikely to build such leaders because of the slow pace of how they work, and Indian entrepreneurs can try developing this capability if there is enough trust in the individual. This capability needs you to rethink feedback, rethink the review system and rethink empowerment.

It's a paradox that I have never seen any company say that they are fast and effective. I have always heard every company say that they are slow but methodical. Every management team thinks it's fast. The true test of a company being fast is if its ecosystem thinks it's fast.

Profit and Profitability

The second important variable to think about in leading a business is profit and profitability.

Profits are always sacrosanct, whether your business is a physical business, a digital business or an omni business. In the last few months, it has become fashionable to say that a digital business is unprofitable. I am certain this is unsustainable, and I don't agree with it.

If you are leading your business well, you will have a good sense of the fixed costs of the business, the variable costs and where you are using up capital. I always ask CEOs to look at costs as what's in their control and what's not in their control. I have seen CEOs debate corporate head office allocations to death, when there is so much more fat sitting in their own system. In most businesses, there is excess inventory in the system, raw material inventory as well as finished goods inventory. I see so many made-to-order businesses holding inventory. Your inventory model must match your business model, as an example—you cannot be a made-to-order business and have ready stock.

Costs are something a good business prunes every year. Look at your business costs as good costs and bad costs. Anything to do with new capability-building is a good cost or investment; anything to do with strengthening fundamentals is a good cost. There are many sophisticated concepts/systems that can help, like activity-based budgeting, zero-based budgeting, etc. I always ask CEOs to cut costs in line with inflation, i.e., they must be inflation-proof year on year. Your costs must remain the same despite inflation or actually drop year on year. This is tough but the only way out when it comes to running a good business.

If your costs balloon, you either have to take price increases, which makes you uncompetitive with someone in the ecosystem, or you have to sacrifice profits, which makes you unpopular with your stakeholders.

When you cut costs, cut the flab but never the muscle in your system. Never cut costs to the bone, which requires you to add back costs later on. The moment Nokia cut its R&D budget, which was absolute core in that sector, Nokia stopped being innovative.

Costs accrue in a system as a result of activity in the system. I would urge you to look at activity in the system and prune it every six months. Activity has a way of growing, like grass and weeds in your garden. In the pandemic, one of the businesses we studied had increased its review meetings from sixteen to twenty-two per month. So, obviously they were incurring extra costs, without realizing it. Even if they were not incurring cash costs, they were incurring time cost and cost of delays and procrastination with everyone at meetings.

Digital systems allow you to discard a number of the old physical processes. Digital processes help integrate across functional boundaries to give you agility and also to help you arrive at one version of the truth in running your business. If you can get to one version of the truth for any important measure in your organization, that will be a powerful point to rally your team to greater success.

Many think that the cost of people in emerging markets is low. That's not true at all. Some of the most expensive middle managers are in Africa. China is no longer a low-wage country. India is low-wage compared to developed economies, but is not matched with high productivity. Low wages with high productivity is good for the business, but low wages with low productivity is terrible for a business. High wages with low productivity nearly killed the US auto industry.

Think about automation in your industry. What can be automated and what cannot be? You can automate your packing line, whether you are a B2C business or a B2B business. We will see robots working along with human beings in factories and offices this decade. If your business is going to do it, you need to rethink policies for employees and productivity norms. Employees have to move up the analysis

Countries That Pivoted, Countries That Didn't

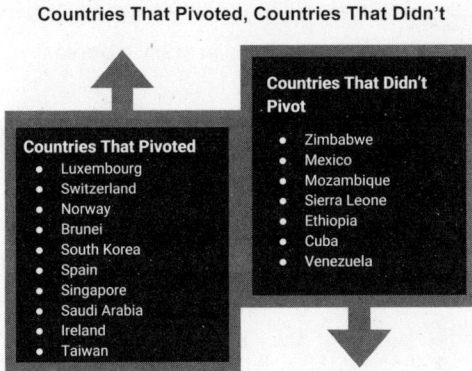

Countries That Pivoted
- Luxembourg
- Switzerland
- Norway
- Brunei
- South Korea
- Spain
- Singapore
- Saudi Arabia
- Ireland
- Taiwan

Countries That Didn't Pivot
- Zimbabwe
- Mexico
- Mozambique
- Sierra Leone
- Ethiopia
- Cuba
- Venezuela

Source: https://www.lovemoney.com/gallerylist/73262/10-countries-that-used-to-be-poorbut-are-now-rich

chain and give you more insights as robots end up crunching the numbers, settling the bills, making the payments, etc.

I predict that robots will first take over hazardous jobs on factory assembly lines, then the heavy-lifting jobs, then the dull and boring repetitive jobs.

Adidas has moved their shoe-manufacturing from China to Germany. This new, automated, fully robotic plant runs with six employees and is one of the largest in the world. Scale is not possible in the future without automation and digitization.

There is always the debate in organizations about absolute profit or percentage profit. I think absolutes matter, and percentages can change over time as long as you are not grossly off the industry or peer benchmark. Any business with less than a 10 per cent EBITDA margin will always be challenged and will have to compete harder to build any sense of competitive advantage. Competitors are always snapping at your heels when you make low profits. So you get into a vicious cycle of low profits/profitability, high price competitiveness, dropping margins, increasing costs and cutting costs.

I would never ask you to sacrifice margins for revenue growth. Those days are over when one could recoup investments with scale, etc., and build physical advantages.

Another way of managing profits is to rethink 'revenue management'. The airlines industry, the hospitality industry, the beverages industry are all good at revenue management as they look at dynamic pricing day in and day out. This is not something that B2B businesses are good at, but they can benefit a lot if they try a few principles of supply with different types of demand. Digital businesses do this by sheer force of habit. I remember my book *The Right Choice* going through price ups and downs as the category managers at Amazon tried to arrive at an optimum mix of volume and profit.

The publishing industry is a funny business. The e-commerce sellers are constantly trying to lower the price points; the publisher replenishes stock but penalizes the author if the stock is unsold; and the poor author is at the receiving end of both the seller and the publisher. So, there are three different people managing the measures differently in managing their businesses for the same product.

Many organizations tend to benchmark 'best practice' versus competitors for cost management. I think they should be driving the next curve of 'next practice' if they want better profitability.

The element of capital expenditure is another aspect to consider. In my experience, capital expenditure proposals are not balanced and rarely deliver on their promised returns. The capital expenditure proposals are either too conservative and pessimistic, or too audacious and overpromising. Capital expenditure proposals overpromise when they know that the normal analysis will not show good returns, and hence the margins, growth, mix are always overstated in such proposals. In running a business, watch this. Capital expenditure proposals are made with 'what the boss wants' or 'what the hurdle rate is for the committee to approve this'. If a business has depreciation at more than 10 per cent, then that's a different problem. PepsiCo India had high capex, which led it to building huge bottling capacities, and the business was chasing its tail to trim it.

There are no holy cows in cost. Take R&D as an example. For years, R&D was a cost centre, till a few companies made it a profit centre. A.G. Lafley of Procter & Gamble made R&D a profit centre. He encouraged his R&D engineers to source patents from outside, sell their patent ideas, etc. By dropping the R&D cost, he spent more on brand-building. Pfizer is doing the same. They have moved into an open R&D system. Many educational institutions with good labs have become partners of this open R&D network in the last few years.

I have seen that people costs creep up whenever a matrix structure multiplies or a central function at headquarters grows. Every line in the matrix wants more people and more oversight. This leaves no one accountable. The funny part of a matrix structure is that each function has its own offsite and learning, sharing meetings in exotic locations. When the country CEO opposes this travel, the matrix says it will bear the full cost, knowing fully well that it gets allocated back to every country. These are silly games that the matrix and its leaders must stop indulging in if they want a competitive cost structure. The power in matrix is in granting people higher job grades and pay structures, and this again defeats the cost argument. Managing costs is a challenge in a matrix organization.

Broad Components of an Effective Leadership Pipeline

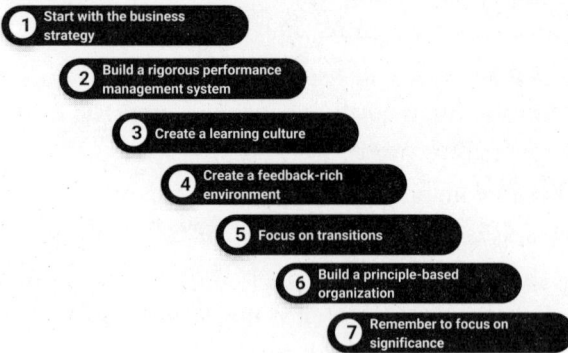

1. Start with the business strategy
2. Build a rigorous performance management system
3. Create a learning culture
4. Create a feedback-rich environment
5. Focus on transitions
6. Build a principle-based organization
7. Remember to focus on significance

Source: https://www.insights.com/media/1104/building-aleadership-pipeline.pdf

Process

The next element in managing a business is process. This becomes important when you are working remotely.

An organization must encourage the framing and efficient running of processes if they want a process culture. Processes are the right enabling link between strategy, business model and daily execution. Process culture is about employee behaviour and attitude to systems and documentation.

Process brings the needed discipline and rigour to run a daily business. I have seen lack of process lead to a 'hero' culture and very variable execution.

Every business has a set of core processes depending on the nature of the business. Most product manufacturing companies have most of the following ten core processes:

i.   Sales and marketing
ii. Innovation
iii. Supply chain or end-to-end value creation model
iv. Procurement/raw materials sourcing
v.   Human resources
vi. Reputation management
vii. Financial analysis
viii.IT
ix. CSR
x.   Collections/receivables

Small companies do not need processes, as everyone chips in and work gets done energetically. An organization needs a structure when its headcount crosses 100, and then you need interlock meetings or SLAs, or coordination meetings or a PMO (project management office).

Process management is again cultural. European and Japanese companies follow process to a T, so much so that they pardon failure as long as the process is followed. Eastern cultures tend to work on personal equations in an organization as opposed to managing a process. Process is seen as limiting, boring, bureaucratic, stifling in Asian cultures.

There are good examples of processes benefiting organizations.

Toyota became competitive when it built its 'Just in Time' management process. This helped them save money, integrate the vendor ecosystem and deliver on time.

Southwest Airlines prides itself on being best in class in turnaround time. They achieved this by mapping all the activities and seeing how each activity adds value or adds time to the objective of aircraft turnaround.

ICICI Bank in India was able to digitize their operations because their processes were tight. This helped them propel to a digital banking system, replacing the more cumbersome physical system.

Nokia nearly collapsed in the early 2000s because of a faulty supply-chain process. Nokia then redesigned it and went to being best in class by managing their supply chain and inventory across three time zones, and calling off needed inventory and excess inventory almost on a bi-weekly basis.

Airlines, digital delivery companies and food delivery companies use digital tracking to estimate arrival time and create value perception. This is a crucial process, a promise that's visible to both the company and the consumer.

The National Transportation Safety Board (NTSB) in the US is an independent federal agency which is charged with investigating every civil aviation accident and any significant events in highway, marine, pipeline and railroad accidents. They do this by being extraordinarily process-focused in ticking every box in terms of the processes the pilots or other responsible people are supposed to follow. If you watch any of the Discovery series on air accidents, you realize the emphasis the NTSB lays on process discipline as it involves human lives. Pilots are expected to check off systematically on every process before they take off and land.

The ecosystem which follows rules and processes 99.9 per cent of the time is the air travel ecosystem between air traffic controllers, pilots and ground crew. There is a manual, rule and process for every activity in this industry.

The security system at every airport around the world after 9/11 is another example of the adoption of a common security code and process discipline.

Framework for Managing/Governing Ecosystem

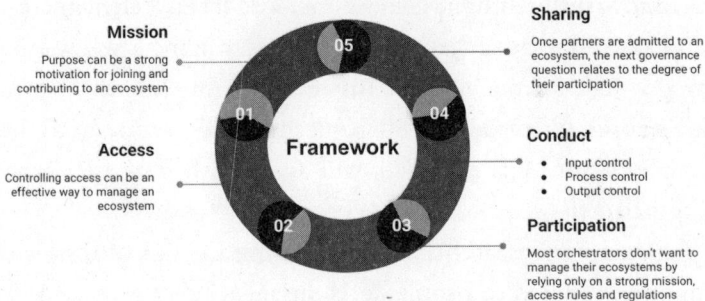

Mission
Purpose can be a strong motivation for joining and contributing to an ecosystem

Access
Controlling access can be an effective way to manage an ecosystem

Framework

Sharing
Once partners are admitted to an ecosystem, the next governance question relates to the degree of their participation

Conduct
- Input control
- Process control
- Output control

Participation
Most orchestrators don't want to manage their ecosystems by relying only on a strong mission, access rules and regulations

Source: https://www.bcg.com/publications/2021/how-to-manage-business-ecosystem

Having sold a billion burgers, Ray Kroc, the founder of McDonald's, once said, 'Yes, we sell a billion burgers, but we make and sell them one at a time.' The QSR (quick service restaurant) industry is an industry where every process needs to be followed. They have their own versions of training universities to enable this standardization. Process discipline gets you high standardization of customer experience.

Another industry where processes need to work is the TV broadcast industry. Things need to work like clockwork if the time schedules through the day are to be met. So, processes are a must-have if you have slim margins and time constraints.

People

The third area in managing a business is people. This is a tough area. It is very difficult to get all people decisions right, be it hiring them, letting them go or promoting them to responsible roles.

How difficult are people decisions? Jack Welch, the ex-CEO of GE, said in an interview that when he was young he got just 50 per cent of his hiring right, but as he rose to become CEO he got 80 per cent of his decisions right. I am not sure GE observers will agree with him after what happened to GE.

American researcher and author Jim Collins offers seven questions related to people decisions:

i. Are you losing other people because you have kept this person in the seat?

ii. Do you have a values problem, a skills problem or a will problem?

iii. What's the person's relationship with windows and mirrors? When a job is well done, does he look out of the window, i.e., look ahead and let his team take the credit? Or does he/she stand in front of a mirror taking credit?

iv. Does the person see work as a job or a responsibility?

v. Has your confidence in the person gone up or down in the last one year?

vi. Do you have a bus problem or a seat problem on this bus?

vii. How would you feel if the person quit?

We used to look at context in hiring people. We would have a safe pair of hands for a steady business, we would want an ambitious person for a fast growth opportunity, etc.

We need people who can execute flawlessly day after day. I think everything around people—recruiting, engagement, training, location, salaries, bonus areas, succession—will be rethought in the coming twelve months and the next few years.

Public Opinion

The fifth element is public opinion. In the past, public opinion was generated by editorials, favourable media reports, awards, etc. Today, the public image is completely dominated by social media. Social media is ecstatic one moment and despondent the next. Your company or brand will have a loyal set of followers who will follow you and be positive about you no matter what you do. But the larger commentary is what you need to worry about.

Recent advertisements from leading brands have been challenged and withdrawn, words and posts by corporate leaders have been challenged with counter-facts and opinions.

Social media adds a positive layer to your customer engagement. Nike is the best practice here.

Social media expands the footprint of your consumer base, mostly in a positive way.

Social media develops unique virality. Small brands benefit most from this, as social media builds rapid awareness.

Social media is more economical compared to most other media channels. When social posts go viral, the cost of that is very economical. The Sri Lankan singer and YouTuber Yohani's song 'Manike Mage Hithe' is a recent example.

Social media increases the pride your employees feel. Employees feel proud when they get favourable social commentary on brand advertising, on company initiatives, etc.

Social media shows your stakeholders that you are willing to listen. By putting out details like your email id, phone numbers, names and contact details of relevant people, you are showing that you are willing to listen. And consumers make use of that by tagging the company or the CEO when there is deviation from the standard. The best examples include delayed flights, poor airline service, poor restaurant service, etc. These grab attention. We also know that a satisfied consumer doesn't really share his/her experience in the same way a consumer with a negative experience does. Research shows that consumers with negative experience tell at least eight other people about their poor experience.

PricewaterhouseCoopers (PwC) released their twenty-fifth annual CEO survey in January 2022. It's a comprehensive look at 2022 and beyond that includes interviews with about 4446 CEOs in eighty-nine countries. Some of the findings are a good barometer for you to think about the coming years.

The top four findings from India:

1. Ninety-eight per cent of Indian CEOs are confident of revenue growth in 2022, and the figure is similar for the year after. This figure has traditionally been high for Indian CEOs. For Global CEOs it is 77 per cent.
2. Eighty-nine per cent of Indian CEOs are concerned about the health impact post the pandemic.
3. Eighty-one per cent of Indian CEOs have put customer satisfaction as a measure in their long-term strategy.
4. Twenty-seven per cent of Indian CEOs have committed to a net zero emissions target.

Lessons from that list: CEOs are getting more consumer/customer-oriented than before—clearly, having a licence to produce is not a licence to sell. Sustainability is gaining ground, and Indian companies are making the moves.

Let's now look at the geographies Indian CEOs see as key for success in their growth plans:

1. Sixty-one per cent pick the USA
2. Thirty-one per cent pick China
3. Twenty-seven per cent pick the UK
4. Seventeen per cent pick the UAE

Lessons from that: Indian CEOs clearly see themselves in an interconnected world. As technology becomes important, USA will be a key country for Indian organizations. China is important and will be important for Indian businesses despite the doubts. I am surprised that Japan and Germany do not figure on that list. This will also have some implications on our trade-bloc priorities.

Here's a long-term strategy measures comparison between Indian CEOs and Global CEOs:

	Indian CEOs	Global CEOs
Customer satisfaction	81%	71%
Employee engagement	75%	62%
Automation/digitization	78%	54%

The top six risks that Indian CEOs see are:

Risk	Percentage
Health risks	89%
Geopolitical risks	77%
Cybersecurity	77%
Macroeconomic risks	75%
Climate risk	62%
Social inequality	45%

Again, this shows the global connectedness of Indian businesses. It is good to see that social inequality is appearing on the list. India has some distance to cover in that area.

Indian CEOs list these five as watchout areas:

i.   Digital and technology finance. The platformization of consumer financial services, regulatory issues, market changes.
ii. Transition to clean energy.
iii. Metaverse.
iv. Mobility and digital collision.
v.   Virtual evolution of health and wellness.

Here again, technology is front and centre. I expect technology and the ability of the organization to pivot to a technology-first approach the single most important factor for success. The world GDP in 2022 is expected to cross $100 trillion for the first time. The top five sectors globally are:

i.   Financial services: $22–23 trillion
ii. Construction: $10.5–12 trillion
iii. Real estate: $10 trillion
iv. E-commerce: $10 trillion
v.   Health and life insurance: $10 trillion

Digital will sweep each of these industries in India too. Digital cuts transaction costs in every industry, digital takes away the inefficient middleman, digital brings in radical transparency, digital helps brands extend into unrelated areas, digital enables the building of a subscription model. There will be privacy issues to be addressed, data authenticity, etc. This will happen with a degree of industry self-regulation and a degree of government regulation.

The shift to digital will have a big impact on the skill set you need in employees. In a changing world, companies will value skills over degrees. We will see an overhaul in education and in the growth of digital skill courses.

Running a successful business will require too many things to work in tandem for a reasonable amount of time. Looking back and trying to run a business is a sure way to fail; looking ahead and building an approach will have a better chance.

Legacy organizations will struggle to change. The fundamental change is that in every sector the consumer has gone 24/7. Consumers want food through the day, they want medicines through the day, they want advice through the day, they want astrology through the day, they want information and entertainment through the day. The first global 24/7 business was the news business, with CNN in 1991; everyone followed suit. Business models will keep evolving. There won't be one way of making a profit in the future.

Hrishikesh Bhattacharyya

Hrishi Bhattacharya worked with Unilever all his life, and is now retired and settled in America. He was director of the beverages division and then became marketing director of Hindustan Unilever India. Subsequently, he did a stint in Brazil before moving to the headquarters of Unilever in a strategy role.

Hrishi was always regarded in Unilever as one of the best structural thinkers and a sharp marketing mind. He has also authored a number of articles with the late C.K. Prahalad. In this interview Hrishi talks about moving consumers from an unorganized sector to the organized sector, the skills needed to be a future marketer, the difference between fads and trends, and how the primary role of a leader is about managing change while that of a manager is about reducing complexity.

You have been involved with a number of strategies at Unilever, including converting unorganized markets to organized markets in tea, soaps and detergents. What are the lessons and watchouts for a business or manager when it comes to upgrading from commodity/unorganized markets?

This conversion task was both a key priority and a big challenge, starting from the mid-'60s to the early '80s. A few different approaches were tried with Lux soap miniatures, Surf sachets, tea paisa packets and shampoo single-use packs. It was only after about ten years of experimentation and practice that we could conceptualize that success required a 'package' of activities. First and foremost was the unit size of the product and its unit price. Second, distribution had to be driven well beyond market wholesaler capabilities. Third, media dark markets were many, and ways had to be found to reach the brand's advertising story. Fourth, reaching prospective consumers and showing them how to use the products and the results they got compared to their current usage required another set of activities. To these ends, we created sales-cum-cinema vans. They would go to remote markets, sell during the day and screen movies after dark. More than 100 of these company-owned and -run vehicles criss-crossed the country. We invented sales-cum-demonstration units, and deployed them in large congregations, like at fairs and festivals. And finally, many hours were spent in home-to-home sampling and also product demonstrations. When this four-pronged operation was done, and done well, we got enormously good results. But it was hard, missionary work.

You have worked in India, Brazil and also worked from the corporate HQ of Unilever. You have seen a wide variety of marketers in your career. Where can Indian marketers be better, and what do they do well?

I worked many years in India, and in my later years visited and interacted with Unilever managers in over forty countries, in all regions of the world. So, this is a good question to deal with. Over the last fifty years, we, in HLL, have been able to recruit the best talent from the best educational institutions in India. As a result, we are, by far, the most educated group of managers starting out in a Unilever company. A lot of our managers also hold double degrees in engineering, chartered accounting and business management, and that is rare too.

Because of this background, our managers are very good with quantitative methods, logic and analysis. Planning in an in-depth way, being competitive and hard work are in their genes. So, they learn fast and do most marketing tasks very well. It is no surprise that our managers are in high demand around the world, at all levels.

Like in many other things, our strengths often lead to certain weaknesses. For example, we tend to extrapolate from the past to the future, and that results in inaccuracy, as, more and more, the future is not like the past. We also have a poor record of launching new, relevant products tailored for our market. With 1.5 billion people in a market, and taking a fifty-plus year view, we can count on the fingers of one hand only five genuinely new products/branding: Dalda, Rin, Fair & Lovely, Wheel and Taaza.

The one trait of Indian managers that I feel unhappy about, not just in marketing, but in all functions and at all levels, is our meekness in front of hierarchy, and easy acceptance of out-of-date rules and regulations. Speaking up when face to face with the boss, even with a good idea in the bag, was, and it probably still is, a rarity.

One of the challenges for any business leader is to differentiate a trend from a fad. We see healthy foods, organic foods, Ayurvedic medicines, Chinese medicines, etc., in front of us. What rules of thumb or framework did you use personally in determining the differences between a fad and a trend?

Fads are important in toys, fashion, music and the diet world. Since I had no experience in any of these businesses, I never became a victim of fads. But trends I have seen. The real tragedy, of course, is when you see a trend after everybody else has seen it, because then it is too late and potential business opportunities have been missed. This happens frequently to excessively data-driven managers, who believe in facts only when the data shows it. Such people always live in the past or the present, but never in the future.

After about ten years of working, my role changed primarily from managing operations to creating and implementing strategy. That was when I seriously started thinking about how to create and shape the future. I played with things like scenario planning, war games, trend lines and so on, and found that none of them work. More thinking and experimentation led to a robust framework. First, you had to think about societal trends and then match them with technological trends for a particular benefit space. In 1974, at age twenty-eight, I found that 'looking fairer was a deep-seated desire in Indian society, especially amongst women'. We, at HLL, had a technological solution, which safely delivered the desired results. Fair & Lovely was born. Today, after almost fifty years, it contributes a huge chunk of the company's profits.

Here is another example. A societal trend is that infectious diseases are giving way to lifestyle disorders. The key health problems facing middle-aged people are: digestive problems, aches and pains, diabetes, sleep disorders, mental stress and so on. Looking at technology, allopathy does not do as well here as it does with infections. But the technology exists. Ancient Indian and Chinese medicines work very well with these lifestyle conditions.

One can also start by looking at technological trends and apply them to customer needs and wants. Staying in the health-care space, one can see that genome sequencing, stem cell research, biosciences and immunology, along with advances in imaging and robotics, can create a totally new medical world. Imagination is all you need now to marry the new science to the patient. One key lesson is that you must look at societal and technology trends outside your industry. Once you get them, try and apply them to your space. Using trends in this way leads to big innovation and profit flows.

One more illustration might help to understand this. A key societal trend today is the desire, among both men and women, for fitness and weight loss. But current methods of delivery do not work. The reason is that the customer has a varied menu of needs which need to come together in an integrated way. Before starting a programme, one requires a benchmark study of current health (and disease) status, which means a physician and a diagnostic laboratory; design of a customized exercise regime, preferably with a personal coach; a dietician to plan and monitor calorie intake, and a balanced mix of food, drink and nutrients; a pharmacy for medicines and supplements; a greengrocer and a packaged-goods grocer, to supply healthy fruits, vegetables and the right proteins; the exercise should take place at home with a different schedule each day, if required; and easy payments for all of this. And so on. That is why fitness and diet offerings do not work and, after some time, cannot be sustained. But can this be delivered? The answer is yes. A digital–physical platform, consisting of a network of high-quality suppliers, covering everything the customer needs and wants, can be designed and implemented. The platform owner brands and holds your credit card. This was actually done for an Indian company in health care when I was working with them as a strategy consultant.

We live in a fast-changing world. How do you see the role of strategy today, and how should strategy adapt to this newer, faster world?

The role of business strategy will actually become more important, but the practice has to get better. Like many commonly used words, strategy is understood in multiple ways, most of them wrongly, leading to uneven results and frustration with the practice.

Many start with strategy development as a first step, and think of it as a means of addressing competition and beating it. The core steps are industry analysis and competition understanding. There are several problems with this. First, strategy is not a starting point; second, it is getting increasingly difficult to define one's industry and also who our competitors are, and whether what's true at present will also be true of the future. Take the case of phones. Does a phone still allow one to make and receive calls? Yes, it does. But it also: shows time (watch), dates and appointments (calendar and diary), sends and receives emails and SMSes (communicator), connects to the Internet (computer), takes photographs and videos (camera), stores and plays music and movies (record player), stores presentations (files, slides), makes deposits and payments (banking), and so on. So, can someone define this industry? Or name its chief competitor?

Based on listening to and reading the experts, and my own five-decade-long association with strategy creation and practice, I believe the following. First, that strategy is indeed a response. But it is a response to your 'Core Purpose' and 'Targeted Future', and not to your current competition. So, what are Core Purpose and Targeted Future? Core Purpose (CP) is the organization's reason to exist. It is an enduring identity that transcends product or market life cycles, technological breakthroughs, management fads and individual leaders. It is internal inspiration—it does not have to be exciting for outsiders. The role of CP is to guide, not to differentiate. Targeted Future is a clearly articulated goal. It is clear, compelling, a unified focal point for effort. It is tangible, energizing, focused and engages people at all levels.

Strategy looks very complex, and many people take many pages to articulate theirs. I practise it in a simple way, by answering four basic questions: Which consumers will I serve? In which markets? With what products and services? How will I win?

Finally, often those who design strategy, do not or cannot get buy-in from their implementors. Big folders and digital files are prepared, which languish in the proverbial drawer. A successful strategy must be capable of being expressed in thirty words.

Here is what I consider a good piece of work done by an Indian company in the health-care space (I was involved with them as a consultant):

Core Purpose: 'Inspiring and enhancing the quality of human life by enabling people to feel better, remain youthful and enjoy an active life.'

Targeted Future: 'Be the pre-eminent player in the treatment of life style related disorders, pioneering collaborative and first-line treatment methods, with a 5000 crore business potential in 10 years.'

Strategy in 30 Words: 'Help 35+ year people manage various stages of life style related ailments through proven primary and complementary natural solutions via an eco-system of doctors and trade to deliver advice and services conveniently.'

A large inter-functional team created and wrote this. The agreed, and board-approved, output was widely communicated to all managers at all levels. Everyone in the company knew the firm's philosophy, what it was seeking to achieve, and every manager also knew that their own activities had to be designed and aligned to this strategy.

You wrote a few articles with C.K. Prahalad on innovation. How do you see the confluence of innovation and the concept of 'bottom of the pyramid' in a digital, post-pandemic world, when the number of the poor has gone up?

Having more poor is an opportunity, not a problem! *The Fortune at the Bottom of the Pyramid* was published in 2004. When C.K. Prahalad was researching and writing it, between 2002 and 2003, the world was a very different place. CK was really trying to establish a principle, and the examples he gave to prove the concept were small gains (paisa packets, shampoo sachets) and essentially low-hanging fruit. In numerous conversations that he and I had at that time, I knew that the opportunity that he imagined was much bigger, and he was absolutely right.

The potential fortune from this customer group is a single product symbol: the cellphone and the smartphone. In

2004, there were only 180 million cellphones in the world, and most of them were in the rich countries. Today, the number of unique mobile subscribers is 5 billion, of which smartphones constitute 4 billion. The interesting question is: Who has these phones? The answer is that China and India have 1.5 billion of them, while USA has just 300 million. So the phones are essentially in the hands of the poor!

What this establishes is that aspiration is driving the poor, that they are capable of buying high-value items, but these have to be suitably designed for reach and purchasing power. Low, frequent payments, like in the case of the 2004 shampoo sachets, is still the game.

What enabling mechanisms have emerged in the last twenty years? The reach of the Internet was 1 billion in 2005—today it is almost 5 billion, in a global population of around 8 billion. In India, for example, electricity is reaching remote villages, and much more can be done with solar power. Broadband Internet is going to reach villages soon. Eighty per cent of Indians have bank accounts—that is more than 1 billion accounts. Add to that microlending and auto-pay systems. So, the technology is present.

As explained in the trends answer, when customer aspirations and technology can be married, new big business opportunities arise. Poverty can be reduced only when skill sets develop—this requires nutrition, hygiene and health, secondary schooling, skill-imparting schooling, pucca housing, etc. These are core societal aspirations at the bottom of the pyramid, and the technology to deliver them exists. In my mind's eye, I can see profitable businesses delivering affordable housing, transportation (electric bicycle), world-class secondary education, basic health care. We have failed C.K. Prahalad so far; but I am sure that imaginative entrepreneurs will now emerge.

What are the skill sets needed of a modern-day marketer and a modern-day CEO?

These are key leadership roles in an organization, and their primary job is to lead. So, how do you define a leader? In all my varied reading on the subject, I think one of the most apt descriptions came from President Bill Clinton. This is what he said in 2004: 'The Job of a President is to understand and explain the time in which he serves, to set forth a vision of where we need to go, and a strategy of how to get there, and then to pursue it with all his mind and heart, bending only in the face of error or new circumstances and the crises which are unforeseen.' What applies to the leader of a country applies equally to the leader of a company. Only the scale of wins and losses differs.

Like all leaders, the best CEOs and CMOs essentially do three things:

(a) Decide what needs to be done
(b) Create networks of people to accomplish the agenda
(c) Ensure that the work actually gets done

The most important thing, to my mind, is that they are simultaneously both leaders and managers. The tasks are full of thinking, planning and, very importantly, execution. In essence, therefore, the CEO and the CMO play a double role—sometimes as a leader and most of the time as a manager. The leader's deliverable is change; the manager's goal is to reduce complexity. As a leader, the CEO creates the vision and the overarching strategy, aligns people and motivates and inspires them company-wide. The CMO, in his leadership role, does the same three things but only for his functional area. Again, as managers, their scope is company-wide, but their tasks and outcomes are essentially the same. They plan and budget to get predictability and orderly results; they design systems for implementing plans and get the right fit between people and jobs; and, finally, they make it easy to complete the jobs. I would say that for the CEO the split between leadership time and management time would be more like 60:40, while for the CMO, or any other functional leader, it would be more like 35:65.

Renuka Ramnath

Renuka is the founder and CEO of Multiples Alternate Asset Management Pvt. Ltd, which she started after a long and illustrious career at ICICI Bank. She is an independent director of the apparel manufacturer Arvind Ltd, and the chairperson of the Tata Communications board.

In this interview Renuka talks about her philosophy of picking entrepreneurs to invest in, how she managed her company in the pandemic and what reputation means in today's investment climate.

You are an entrepreneur. How do you plan your business for a future world? What variables do you consider and what do you drop?

If we're talking about sectors, then obviously our industry is famous for picking futuristic sectors with aggressive growth characteristics, or sectors that are significantly disruptive in nature. That way you can invest in companies which are disrupting incumbent businesses and are therefore going to have an aggressive growth path.

There are two fundamental pillars on which we evaluate our investment. One has to do with the macro characteristics of the investment, which tell us about the overall profit pool and revenue pool of the opportunity. And then there are a whole host of other macro factors, such as the competitive landscape, pricing power, extent of government interventions and the ability to build a moat. Next, we look at the team. Is the team thinking about scale, about professionalizing and institutionalizing? Is the team thinking about good governance? Is the team capable of bringing high-quality people and allowing them to perform? So the entire evaluation of the team is probably even more important than the evaluation of the macros.

The ones we do not touch include companies with a blemished past or which have lost their relevance. So, if the company has a past of bad governance, bad attitude or poor conduct with people, we simply drop them. As investors, we assess how big the company can become tomorrow.

Is there a sector that's a completely no-go area for you?

Yeah, of course. For example, all these manufacturing sectors where there are no big moves or which are with fragmented manufacturing. Or services companies with very narrow margins, where the value addition is very marginal. We don't even look at them. We don't touch infrastructure, real estate or any business that requires a government concession. We typically don't like asset-intensive businesses; we prefer knowledge-intensive businesses. Then there are a lot of proprietary businesses, which come to us for 100 per cent buyout. We don't do that. Because if you were to convert a proprietary business into an institutional business, the cost will completely eat up all the profits. So what we look at are scalable businesses, which have attractive profit pools with no government interference and which are knowledge-intensive, not asset-intensive.

How has the pandemic impacted your business, and how are you planning differently for the future?

Initially, I really thought that all hell had broken loose. I thought a lot of my companies would collapse. But it eventually taught us how agile our entrepreneurs are and how robust their business models are. All of my companies have emerged stronger than when they entered the pandemic. So, it has confirmed my belief that adversities are great opportunities for good management. And as the private equity industry, we choose the best of the best, right? So, the pandemic only made our industry stronger, because our companies were clearly the winners. Weaker companies suffer more in adversity, while the strong ones become even stronger. The pandemic also sort of redefined the limits of adaptability, and frankly, it has been an eye-opener for me.

Anything you would do differently in the post-COVID world?

About 4–5 years back, we had added one more element to our toolkit for evaluation—and that is how technologically and digitally savvy the company is. And if they are not, can we build it? Do they have an open mind, or the ability to integrate technology? We had added it into our toolkit as one of the criteria, but today we have to be sure about these aspects before we touch the company. That is the biggest change we have made post pandemic.

Any business or sector that gave you a setback?

Retail businesses, which are completely shopping mall-dependent, are closed. But it is not a setback. This is because we have a strong conviction that the businesses we have chosen to invest in have a strong consumer value proposition, and when things open up, we will have people back in our stores and back in our cinemas. So I am not retail-averse or physical business-averse merely because of the pandemic. The pandemic has accelerated the digital wave. But if you want to go out to a restaurant with a bunch of friends or your family, that is not changing. I mean, you won't say, 'Let's just order on Swiggy and be done.' So, my belief is that experiential retail is not going away.

Your business depends on having high-value talent in the team. How do you judge that?

We have a whole host of questions for which we seek answers around strategic agility. One is about professionalization—the ability to work with other professionals and reward them. One is about attitude towards capital. Another is about attitude towards partnership, because we don't think of ourselves as financial investors; we think of ourselves as genuine business partners. So, if someone is just looking for capital, we are not an appropriate investor in that situation. And then the attitude towards governance. There are a lot of questions that we have to answer before we get satisfied and select a team that we want to work with.

What happens in case the team does not shape up?

There will be no perfect team. So, our next level of evaluation is what is the job on hand and what characteristics does the team have to show. We have a very clear understanding of that . . . Suppose you are building a digital platform, but you have not shown extraordinary agility, out-of-the-ballpark agility, then we will not invest. But if you have not shown that much respect for capital, or whatever, then we evaluate if we can make you learn that and if you are even open to learning.

How do you build business reputation and personal reputation in the financial services industry?

We have to have a very deep understanding of the sector and the business. That's why we invest a lot in building that sector expertise. And we also bring in real sector experts to guide us very practically on what it takes to build a business in the particular sub-sector that we are investing in. The moment you do that, you engage with the entrepreneurs at a very different level. You don't ask questions only around the P&L; you have very subtle and pertinent questions around the challenges of getting scale, challenges of unethical behaviour, challenges of building a team, and so on and so forth. So you build a very deep connection with the entrepreneur who really enjoys talking to you, because you are not only focused on profit and valuations but also on how to strengthen the company. That is one way we build the reputation of being a highly desirable partner. Post investment as well, we have a deep engagement to know exactly where the shoe bites, so that we don't face the classic problem of 'eat the cake because there's no bread'. So we try very hard to be the entrepreneur's delight and engage differently with them depending on their own personalities.

Beyond this, there has to be consistency of conduct, and there has to be respect for the word. You cannot ever go back on what you have promised—there has to be a commitment to saying my company comes ahead of my investment. So I will never do anything to protect my investment which can harm the company; the company always comes first.

So, delivering on the promise of being consistent, being honest, being transparent, being dependable, being knowledgeable, being networked, always prioritizing the purpose over your money and doing it for over forty years—that's what builds a personal reputation as far as I am concerned.

Has there been an instance where your heart wanted to invest in some company that didn't check all the boxes?

It is more often that our mind wants to invest and our heart tells us that something is amiss. If our heart wants to invest, by and large, we go ahead with that. If there are some missing pieces, we figure them out and fix them, because we are comfortable with the team. But sometimes, a business checks all the boxes, but your heart says, 'Something is not right.' It has happened multiple times. Earlier, we used to waste time trying to figure out why there is a heart–mind conflict. Now I say that we have no time to waste. If your heart says no, don't do it.

What lessons have you learnt from watching entrepreneurs Multiples has invested in?

One of the things which has helped us a great deal is our belief that you should be a rock-solid partner behind an entrepreneur who has already gone through so many of your filters and has set up a great business. My learning is that if you empower such entrepreneurs and give them wings, their imagination gets unlocked in ways you cannot imagine at the time of making the investment. So you invariably build a much bigger, much more valuable, much more scaled and sustainable company than the one you entered. I have seen this 100 out of 100 times. And that's what we want to hone as the core deliverable of Multiples.

R.S. Subramanian

R.S. Subramanian, or 'Subbu' to his friends, is the senior vice president and managing director of DHL Express India. Subbu spent years at HUL, honing his sales and marketing skills. He is a graduate of IIM Bangalore.

In this interview Subbu talks about the reasons DHL is no. 1 in the 'great places to work at' list and his style of managing by walking around and developing ICCC, 'Insanely Customer-Centric Culture', at DHL. He also looks at the future of robotics in his business and what it means for the industry.

DHL has consistently been on the 'best companies to work for' list. What have you specifically done for DHL to remain on this list?

Open communication and feedback, shared values and focus on continuous improvement typify DHL culture. We are very consistent about our basics and like to keep things simple. The basic messaging is simple and consistent enough to become second nature for the team. You pick a random DHL person on how they do things, and you may be surprised to find that the answers are about 90 per cent similar.

About ten years ago, we reduced our one-page document on guiding principles or value statements to just two words: respect and results. Respect means you will respect the individual, the environment, the governing laws and local frameworks, while focusing on delivering results. We have three key stakeholders: employees, customers and investors. We want to be an employer of choice; we will provide quality and therefore be a provider of choice for our customer. And we'll deliver benchmark returns for the investors and will be an investment of choice for them.

We focus a lot on fundamentals and train every single DHL employee through our Certified International Specialist (CIS) programme about the DHL way of working. Over the years, this training programme has become a sort of culture-building programme, and it covers everyone—right from a front-line courier to the global CEO.

We've been in the top-ten list of 'best companies to work for in India' for the last five years—and became No. 1 in 2021. This award is not for the company but belongs to every single employee; they have earned it. It means that our team members feel more satisfied than those in any other comparable company. It has been a ten-year climb. Over the years we worked on improving the office infrastructure and workplace hygiene, and gave visibility to our personnel policy. Meritocracy, transparency, communication quality were issues we focused on. You need to improve communication, make the framework clear, well understood and mandated for all—be it managers, supervisors or front-line teams.

Apart from that, there is huge focus on leadership at all levels. We have a training platform for leaders, Certified International Managers (under the CIS umbrella). It covers a wide range of topics for leaders, to train them to provide 'twenty-first-century leadership'.

Our focus on employees is also clear from the fact that even during the pandemic, we did not lay off even a single person globally. We focused first on what is good for the people, then on what is good for the customer. Motivated employees provide great service quality, and therefore the customers are loyal to us. Profit is an outcome. This is the crux of what we call the Focus Strategy, which has been the driver of DHL's success in the last decade.

How did you handle COVID, and what did you need to do in that period? What processes or activities did you discontinue after COVID? What new processes were added?

A few things we had to bring in right away. Reviewing and tightening our business continuity plans, use of PPE, the discipline of maintaining social distancing and heightened cleanliness of our facilities. We had to schedule 1–1.5 hours between shifts for the sanitization of facilities. This also helped us ensure that the teams in different shifts did not meet each other.

Our business runs on physical movement of goods, and we needed a large portion of our operations team members

(1800 out of 3200) to be at work, while the rest of the 1500 team members needed to be working from home. This was something we had never imagined. All functional processes had to be rewired to work from home and most activities became digital double quick. We had to equip our people with desktops/laptops, connectivity and support systems at home. Our people ensured that all the transitions were seamless.

Supervisors called every single employee every morning to check whether they had any problems with themselves or their family members, and if so, immediately got them help and support. This ensured that we were fast to support and also kept the team closely knit.

As a CEO, how do you plan the short-term, medium-term and long-term aspects of this business?

We make a five-year plan for the business. Within that we make annual plans, and within the annual cycle we make a monthly rolling outlook. This plan drives the outlook on the capacity and resources needed. The business plan drives infrastructure requirements, resourcing requirements and the network capacity assessment and so on. However, our investments are obviously made with a longer-term outlook. For example, our largest facility in India recently went live in Bangalore—a 1,00,000 sq. ft facility like that can be built with a ten- or sometimes twenty-year outlook. So investment horizons can be different when we create infrastructure, but the trigger comes from the business plan and the outlook.

What about capex? How do you manage the capex for this business, and how do you prioritize it?

All our capex is geared to support service quality and business growth. I explained about capex planning already. Our investments are typically in infrastructure (facilities, equipment, vehicles and air capacity), digitalization and automation of processes, and the skilling for our people. Capex is always to support growth and quality . . . Our investments have been consistent over the years—we have invested and expanded every year over the last ten years, including 2020 and 2021.

What's the ecosystem of DHL like? And as the leader, how much interaction do you have with that ecosystem, and how do you engage with it?

There are multiple stakeholders we work with, the biggest being our employees and our customers. We believe that DHL has what we call ICCC: Insanely Customer-Centric Culture. Everything we do is for the customers. Our aim is to keep them at the centre of everything we do.

Other big stakeholders are the regulatory agencies and policymakers who define the framework under which our business operates—customs, civil aviation, etc. And DHL is committed to sustainability goals, and that broadens the ecosystem we engage with and operate in.

My engagement with employees follows a firm calendar. I am face to face with all people managers once a month, with a monthly team brief. And we usually have a town hall schedule (about sixty in a year) that gets me the opportunity to meet every employee at least once a year. In addition, we have several engagement opportunities—training programmes, where I am a facilitator, internal conferences and celebration events.

Customer engagements are of two kinds: planned visits/meetings with top customers and customer events. We have an STTT (Straight to the Top) process, whereby any customer can reach me directly in case of service or other issues. I get to face 'chin music' but also get first-hand feedback and opportunity to solve the problem.

I am the vice chairman of the Express Industry Council of India (EICI), a management committee member of the Indo–German Chamber of Commerce and also an active member of the CII committees (logistics, skill development, etc.). These platforms give me the opportunity to engage with the industry, regulators and policymakers when needed.

How do you drive diversity and inclusion (D&I) as a CEO?

D&I is a big area of focus for the group globally. In India, our focus is on gender, geographic and demographic diversity. The ambition is to have diversity in general and to build it in leadership levels too.

The logistics industry traditionally has been a male-dominant business, but the significant changes in the nature of the businesses, due to technology, automation and digitalization, in recent years have opened up the field and also the minds.

Our gender diversity is at 17 per cent outside of operations teams. We have now stepped up our ambition to build diversity in the operations team and also build our overall female employee levels to 30 per cent-plus levels.

This being an organization with a high percentage of supervisor and manager positions filled from within, my focus is to drive diversity at the entry levels. And for lateral recruitment opportunities we will look to ensure diversity in the candidates screened for recruitment. As a CEO, my focus is to give the D&I theme the business mandate, build it into a key action theme for the leaders and create conversation within the organization to change mindsets, eliminate bias in thought and practice, and help create success stories.

How do you manage the talent pipeline in your business? How do you handle people who are good but have failed to deliver results for a year or two?

We have a well-articulated, structured, transparent performance appraisal and assessment system in place, and there's also well-articulated succession planning. So, my personal philosophy is that performance will give you bonuses, but your potential will get you promotions.

Our focus is to help our team members succeed, and develop competencies and skills to grow in the organization. We have an Open Job Posting system that enables visibility and opportunity for all. We encourage cross-functional and cross-divisional moves within the group to help talented people realize their potential.

Underperformers get into a performance improvement plan cycle. Job fitness is reviewed and rotation encouraged to match role and skill set. If there is a skill gap or a competency gap, we impart training or provide projects so that you can build skill and competency. There is significant emphasis on coaching on the job—to help employees develop with support from managers. If repeated coaching and inputs don't improve performance, the person invariably exits the organization. High-performance culture requires us to manage underperformance respectfully too. Performance is important, and people know that.

As a CEO, how do you manage to balance the interests of the local/regional organization and of the global corporation?

We have a fantastic alignment between the country/regional and global organizations. We have never felt at odds with the global corporation. The network nature of our business requires us to work together to deliver global performance for the business and service quality for our customers across the different countries we operate in. As a network business we need all the countries in the network to deliver consistent quality for our customers. So there is significant alignment in philosophies, infrastructure creation, technology deployment and standardization of processes and practices. DHL aims to be world-class everywhere!

How do you plan innovation in your business? Can you give us a few examples of successful innovation that you pioneered?

Our innovations happen in the area of robotics and how you handle shipments. There is a lot of innovation in simplification of processes and driving automation. For example, in 2019 we created service points where a customer can walk in and book a shipment. But then we found we had 250-odd service points across the country where you can walk in and tender a shipment. It's a high-overhead, asset-intensive operation. So we've tried working with franchisees. Then one team member came up with an idea saying, let's get into the 'phygital' model, which is that we give a QR code to a shop. If you ship-scan here, a DHL person will come to pick up your shipment. Now, we have some 3500 outlets or pick-up points.

How do you handle your management team meetings?

I believe in the phrase 'burn shoe leather'. What it means is that instead of calling up a colleague who is in office, I usually walk up to the person. I get the work done in two minutes, which might have taken ten to complete over the phone. Also, I am known to barge into meetings. Somebody I need to speak to is sitting with three people in a meeting. I just open the door, poke my head in and ask my question. This is my style. They do that to me too—and that's fine. So the culture is very informal.

What advice would you give a younger Mr Subramanian who might be starting off right now?

I would suggest that he focus on a few things that I lacked early on. Though the world is very different now, one has to systematically cultivate some perspectives to be stronger for the future.

First, build external orientation—it helps you get the big picture. It's important. Learn to notice problems around you and think of solutions, because that will help in developing opportunities for yourself. With external orientation, you start seeing things, their connections, how the world is working. And that helps you spot problems and find solutions.

The second thing is to learn the basics of economics and commerce early. Given the choice, I will include it in the early-school curriculum. This conditions your mind and gives you a practical view to life.

Learning to manage personal finance and investments is equally important. These learnings came to me a bit late in life. Had they come early, it would have been better.

Harpreet A. De Singh

Harpreet was the first woman pilot hired by Air India. She progressed through the ranks to become the first woman to lead Alliance Air and is now the executive director of Air India.

In this interview she talks about the challenges of being a path-breaking woman in the aviation sector, driving punctuality in Alliance Air and managing revenues in running a business. She also introduces her mantra for being a good human being: PSQ, pure soul quotient.

You were the first woman pilot to join Air India. How did you manage the pressure and the expectations? And what helped you progress successfully?

Actually, I wanted to join the Indian Air Force, but I could not because it was not open to women in 1985. So I decided to join an airline. The challenge actually started from day one, when I made the decision that I wanted to fly. And then I looked around and saw there were no women in the field.

Fortunately, I was in the army and air wing of the NCC [National Cadet Corps], and I had already started flying in the Andhra Pradesh Flying Club. I also commanded the guard of honour for Prime Minister Rajiv Gandhi, though it was not usual for a woman to lead the command. Because of all these experiences, I got a scholarship for my flying training for CPL in IGRUA. I went to Hisar for my private pilot licence before joining IGRUA. I was the only woman there, and there was no accommodation or facilities for women at the flying club. It was tough, but I managed, and for that the credit goes to my parents, especially my father, a former IAF officer, who brought me up in an environment where there was no difference between a boy and a girl.

I rented a house in Hisar, and it was far away from the club. My daily commute on my moped was long and unsafe—the roads were dark and deserted. That was the mid '80s, when there was no way to connect with the family in case I got stuck somewhere; there were no mobile phones. I would constantly keep chanting prayers all the way. I come from a spiritual family, and I have always believed that my power and strength come from the Almighty. In fact, I used to sleep with a knife under my pillow to protect myself in case the need arose. But I was determined to overcome those issues.

After getting the licence, I got selected by Air India as the first woman pilot, which threw me into the limelight. But I never got carried away by it, thanks to my spirituality, which has always kept me grounded and helped me deal with both the highs and the lows. Soon after joining the airline, I was hit by a blow when I got medically grounded on the basis of a little-known test and lost my licence to fly. They said there was a one-in-a-million probability that if I faced lightning of a certain level I would black out. After having fought several odds and financial issues to reach that position, this development was devastating and disappointing. I knew this had something to do with destiny. Then I left for the US, and got a flying licence and a ground instructor's licence. I also discovered that the medical research because of which I had lost my flying licence was being followed only in India and nowhere else in the world.

So I came back to India and rejoined Air India as a pilot trainer against a fresh advertisement. I had two careers in Air India. Again, I was the only woman in the training department, and I was just twenty-five. That meant my peers and my students looked at me with disbelief, and I had to work on their lack of confidence in me. Soon, they came around and realized that I was thorough and knew my stuff. That was how I became the first woman pilot instructor. It was quite a journey.

You are the first woman to head an airline in India. How did you feel when you got selected? And how are you handling the weight of expectations?

By being thorough in everything I do and continuing to learn new things. I realized that to grow in a career and earn people's respect, you need to learn that you have to always keep learning. So, every time there was an opportunity I just took it, even if nobody wanted to do that work. And slowly, my knowledge base expanded to a level where I was writing books for pilots, as well as airline manuals and SOPs. Gradually, I came into a management position. So, from being the first woman pilot who was also the first woman ground instructor, I became the first woman to head the quality management division.

Since I had upgraded my skills as an auditor, I started auditing the entire airline. I then got promoted and became the executive director of in-flight services. Eventually, I became the first woman to head the flight safety systems department, a DGCA-approved post which grants you the power to decide who is fit to fly and who isn't. People started accepting me when they got to know I was being fair and knowledgeable and that I wasn't going to take sides.

Then I became the first woman safety investigator and got involved with the Aircraft Accident Investigation Bureau. I was one of the key persons, instrumental in getting the Star Alliance certification for Air India. So, at that point, I was migrating and integrating the airline's SOPs to meet the Star Alliance requirements and was a member of the Star Alliance Safety Board and Star Alliance Emergency Response Board. So, I almost had a full 360-degree experience in airlines.

COVID started as soon as you took over as the CEO of Alliance Air. How did you have to think about your business with COVID? How did you manage the health and hygiene aspects of the airline in COVID times?

COVID was a different kind of challenging situation. But we adapted really quickly to it. First, we ensured strict adherence to our safety operating procedures, which included social distancing, web check-in, no in-flight catering, PPEs for our cabin crew. That was why we could happily state that we never lost anyone from our crew or from our people working in the airline. The back-office guys had to work from home for some time, and we had to adapt to the totally new way of doing things. I knew that I was not going to ask anyone to come to the office unless I could do it myself. I was the first one to go to the office, and then the others came, slowly. The second COVID wave was surprising, but we were better prepared.

The business shift was that we could start a lot of cargo operations, which was not our initial focus from Air India. We went into China, and we got our Indian evacuees from there, and I remember Air India brought passengers, equipment, oxygen generators and stuff like that, while Alliance Air carried them to the small cities.

As far as the health and hygiene of the staff are concerned, we made sure that the cabin crew and pilots got themselves tested before every flight. Even though it was not mandatory by the regulator, we invested in that, to protect them and their families, because it was so new to everyone. In the initial days, the diagnostic costs were high, but we did not care about that. Safety was of paramount importance.

Punctuality is an important parameter in the aviation industry. How do you, as CEO, drive a sense of punctuality?

Alliance Air has a punctuality score which is around 92–95 per cent, which is very high. We are much higher compared to many other carriers. And we lose out only due to weather. So, flights do get delayed, but by and large we have a good track record of punctuality. In order to make punctuality a cornerstone of our operations, I start with myself and always reach office much before time . . . I encourage my staff to start reacting and reporting things which can cause even one minute of delay. I think with this kind of synergy, we really improved our on-time performance, considering that we are a small operator and going to such unique airfields, where the weather and other reasons can be really challenging. I think they're doing pretty well. But having said that, we shouldn't be complacent. We have to aim for 100 per cent.

I follow a simple philosophy for time management. It's called the Four D's. Whatever only you can do, you only have to do it. So 'do' it, because nobody else can do that for you. Second, anything that you can delegate, you should 'delegate'. The third is, anything that you don't have to do immediately, you can 'delay' it. And anything that doesn't fit into these top three, just 'dump' it.

How do you look at your business in terms of the time frame? What do you plan for in the short term, what in the medium term and what in the long term?

If you don't have a clear vision of what your short-, medium- and long-term priorities are, you will never be a good decision-maker. Let me start with the long term first, because if your long-term goals are unclear, your short-term goals won't be right. Our long-term vision is very clear: we have to connect all two-tier and three-tier cities in the country, and mobilize every airport which is not operational today, by giving them the confidence that Alliance Air can operate. In the long term, we need more aircraft, we need to connect more cities, and we need to have the vision to go to the remotest corner of India in accordance with the Regional Connectivity Scheme. The idea is to enable even an underprivileged citizen of the country to fly. In the medium term, we need to have a five-year plan: If today we have eighteen aircraft, how do I take it to at least twenty-five? I have to move; if I don't put capacity there, we will get finished, because there is competition too. And my short-term plan is to firstly concentrate on the divestment from Air India because it's so entangled in the parent entity that it can't be on its own. About 90 per cent of the work in this regard has been done. I've already drawn out the plan for the next five years, and I'll be handing it over to my successor.

What do you do as a CEO to stay engaged with your people and to motivate them?

I relate to myself as nothing but a simple, pure soul. And I look at every employee around me as a pure soul. So I've always believed in three elements. Besides your IQ, you need an EQ, but most importantly you need a 'PSQ', pure soul quotient. You need to relate to people, you need to make them feel motivated to work with you. They need to be happy too, because that's when you get good results . . . I don't even think I am working for Alliance Air or Air India. I just think I am working for God and that this is my role in this world's drama. That way you don't get affected by the ups and downs; you just take them as part of life. You enjoy your work and keep giving your best. Plus, I don't think I am a CEO. That is the starting point. The moment you go on that ego trip, people refuse to open up and communicate. Don't be attached to the chair—you are only a trustee of that position.

The other thing is that we meditate together frequently, which keeps us focused, calm and energized. In that state of mind, people come up with better ideas, better solutions, because they're in a different space. But you need to do it frequently, because people again go back to their old selves.

The other thing is connecting with the employees. Take middle management, for example. They play an important role. They know what's happening at the front line, and they also know what the senior management wants. But often, they hold on to information and are reluctant to escalate. If middle management is not motivated enough to do the right thing, they can be the biggest stumbling block. So I realized that you have to break these barriers of senior, middle and front line. I address the entire airline online, and go to meet the front-line staff and ask them to find out if they are facing any issues. We then encourage the middle management to bridge the gap.

Then there is senior management and the infighting. When one person comes and tells me something negative about the other person, I call the second person to find out what's going on in the presence of the first person. And I tell them we are not going to leave this room till we sort out the issues.

The other thing is transparency. My office is an open office—anyone can walk in with a suggestion, a comment or criticism. As a leader, I have myself told my team numerous times: please feel free to tell me that I am wrong. If there's a decision that I am making and there's something which I may have missed out on, please point it out so that I can make an informed decision.

The airline business is challenged for profitability. How do you manage the levers of profitability?

All airlines have very thin margins but huge fixed costs. When I took over as Alliance Air CEO, it was like there was zero revenue—just a few crores coming in, which are peanuts. My biggest challenge was how to increase the revenue while keeping costs down. Then we took a bold decision to operate into new sectors. People were wondering why I got into new sectors, especially during COVID. We introduced Mysore, Mangalore, Mumbai–Goa, Bilaspur, Jabalpur, Gorakhpur, etc. And then I realized that the more we operated, some revenue started coming back. At least my aircraft was not parked in the hangar. And I think that paid off, because I managed to increase the revenues considerably.

How do you and your team think of innovation in your business? Is aviation a difficult industry for innovation?

You have to innovate every day. You have to think of doing things differently all the time. If you think this is the way it is, you're going to get wiped out. I've told my staff, 'Now is the time when you're branching out. Forget the legacy issues. You do things differently, get the best in terms of technology and find modern ways of dealing with situations.' And that has to come from the top. The leadership has to promote innovation and keep an eye on what's going on in the industry. There are a lot of start-ups with a lot of new ideas. For example, in a remote airfield, I wanted a hangar. But the question came: Why do I need to invest in making such a big hangar? I want a flexible hangar which can fold up and then fold down, depending on whether an aircraft is there or not. We need this kind of out-of-the-box thinking. That's how you innovate.

What advice would you have for future women leaders?

To be honest, when I am at work I don't think I am a woman. I only think I am a pure soul. However, as a woman, you not only use your intelligence but also use your ability to connect emotionally. Women are naturally designed that way. They should use that to their advantage, take care of the employees and take care of their people. I've never played the woman card, and I don't like it when women do that.

How do you build pride among employees and the ecosystem when you are a small airline pitted against larger airlines?

As far as Alliance Air is concerned, I build that pride by telling them, 'Look, Air India is going to get disinvested soon. You are the ones who are going to be the Government of India's airline. You are the national carrier. Think of yourself with pride. Think of the *tiranga* [tricolour] flying when you are going to that remote city, the pride with which you connect to those people, think you're doing it for the nation . . .' I try to invoke those kinds of feelings in them, because I can see that their body language changes after that. And I genuinely feel that way myself, too.

Anything specific that you do when you have your executive team meetings? You have said group meditation. Anything else?

I encourage them to practise mindfulness. Before I start the meeting, I tell them, 'Let's start with the best thing that happened to you yesterday.' I am very much into all this, maybe because I have also been a trainer. And I think with openness and with no prejudice against anyone. I think my career path has helped me in my role as a CEO.

Olli-Pekka Kallasvuo

Olli-Pekka, or OPK, as he is popularly known, is from the legal domain. He went on to be the CFO and then the chairman and CEO of Nokia. He was also the chairman of Nokia Siemens. OPK chaired the committee for World Design Capital Helsinki in 2012. He has also written a book on his personal journey.

In this interview OPK talks about the non-hierarchy culture in Nokia, its benefits and challenges, the ways of working in a matrix organization and the benefits of any reorganization.

You were the CFO and then the CEO of Nokia. You were closely involved in shaping Nokia into a mobile phone company from being a bits-and-pieces electronics company. When did you and your team realize that Nokia could be big in mobile phones? What signals led you to bet everything on the mobile phones space?

That was in the early 1990s. With the benefit of hindsight, I can say it was an obvious decision, but it was far from straightforward at that time. But there were not too many alternatives that Nokia had; this was the lifeline, and we went for that!

Nokia had many businesses at the time, and it was really diversified as a conglomerate. But many of its businesses were either struggling or were not global in nature. And in that way, it was kind of natural to concentrate on telecommunications or mobile phones, because they seemed to have the best possibilities for success. So we decided to concentrate on something that was smaller, at the time, but had opportunities. And it turned out to be bigger than we expected.

Nokia invested ahead of the curve in R&D. It was always among the top five innovative companies and came out with a string of innovations. When did this thinking emerge—to invest ahead of time in R&D?

In the mobile phone business, you could add value in two ways—through R&D on the one hand, and through brand/marketing on the other hand. In R&D you almost, by definition, have to invest ahead of the curve because basic technology-development cycles are quite long. If you then get the sales success, you can invest more and be continuously ahead of the competition. That was what Nokia did.

You, as the CEO, invested in building the China and India businesses in the late '90s and early 2000s, and both went to be market leaders and key to Nokia's success. What was your thinking when you decided to invest in both India and China? Many people would pick one of them, rarely both.

Nokia's market share had peaked above 40 per cent. It would have been impossible to be on that level without being strong in both India and China. The two markets of course are very different, especially when it comes to distribution and marketing, but to a great extent the R&D investment for both of these markets was common.

What would you do differently if you were to start as the CEO of Nokia all over again?

In fact, I don't think about it at all. Decisions in business are made based on what you know at the time. Too much second-guessing is not in my nature. This is not in contradiction with the fact that of course everyone needs to learn from the past in order to develop.

Nokia was famous for restructuring the organization frequently. In hindsight, did this benefit the organization or hamper it from attaining some stability?

Ideally, one should not reorganize too easily and too often. Sometimes one needs to live with the current structure, albeit it might not be ideal in every respect. As far as Nokia is concerned, it did not happen that frequently while I was there, though it's true that reorganizations did happen, and they took a lot of time and energy. It was done in 2004, 2006 and 2008. In 2006, it was simply due to my becoming the CEO, and as a consequence of that some other management team members were appointed to some different tasks. So I don't think you can call that a reorganization in the right sense of the word. Then, in mid-2008, there was a real reorganization when the management structure of the company was changed to matrix. And the reason for the switch was to develop the company in a way so that the software and services elements were more tightly integrated with the hardware part of things. At that time, the software and apps platform started becoming more and more valuable, and it could not be developed without having a strong link to the development of the devices themselves. This reorganization brought us better integration, better economies of scale and muscle, though it's true that we lost a bit of speed and agility, which usually happens in a matrix structure. So you need to look at both the aspects of a change. Nothing is black and white here. So, one reorganization happened in 2004 and the other in 2008. Not too many, you see.

In your opinion, what was Nokia's biggest strength, and what were its areas of improvement as a culture?

The biggest strength and the biggest weakness, when it came to the culture, were in fact two sides of the same coin.

While the non-hierarchical, empowering and sharing way of working was a great benefit and source of inspiration and a lot of energy, it also sometimes led to indecision and the weakening of the feeling that individuals had a responsibility. In such situations, individuals don't make decisions; teams and meetings start making decisions. If there's a 'meeting' making the decision, there will be several opinions, and as a result, it becomes difficult to reach a consensus on anything. And without consensus, nothing happens. On the other hand, if there's an individual who firmly believes he or she has to make this decision, then obviously something happens—right or wrong, but at least it happens. With too many people being involved, which is great, energizing and inspiring, decisions might not be made. And that's what I feel was the downside.

You led a unique exercise in developing the company values of Nokia by asking people to send in their suggestions through more than fifty value cafés globally, which led to a presentation by the employees on what Nokia's culture should be. The team then developed a values song written by Billie Hartless, and that became the song that spread the company-values message across Nokia. What led to this empowerment of the employees to decide the Nokia values?

Yes, the exercise was global and very much carried out by the employees, not directed from the top at all but of course facilitated.

It all started when at some point the management team began to say: 'We have been speaking of the same values for fifteen years now. Do people believe in them? Do they resonate with the employee base?' And then it was a joint decision by the team to look at whether the values felt right to our employees. Subsequently, there were these facilitated meetings in various parts of the world where employees discussed the values—what values we had then as opposed to fifteen years before. A lot of discussion took place globally. The employees then selected representatives to do regional meetings about this. And it then culminated in a global meeting in Helsinki for 2–3 days, where people discussed and came up with the values.

How easy or difficult is it to lead a brand and a company in a fast-changing technology sector? What were your learnings?

Nokia was in a B2C, fast-moving consumer goods business, where the cycles are fast and where you need to win the consumers' hearts and minds time and time again. This is not easy, and there aren't many companies that have succeeded in that long term. It's not easy to be a leader both in technology and in branding and marketing, and to succeed you have to excel in both. So, it's very complex. If you can do both at the same time, very well. And this was what Nokia did for a long time. But it's difficult to excel on a continuous basis in both.

You invested your life in Nokia. How do you feel now, looking at Nokia from the outside at this stage?

The company and the work there gave so much to me. I had the privilege to be a part of that for thirty years, and it makes me feel very humble. Basically, everyone I worked with at Nokia during my tenure is no longer there. So I really don't know what's happening now. But the company is not only the people who are working there; it's much deeper than that, and the history runs through the company. It's like a knife which is the same, though its blade and handle have been changed many times. So that's what I feel with Nokia. Same company, even though the blade and the handle have been changed many times. Nokia is not in the phone business any more. And that simply is an illustration of how things can change tremendously. I feel it's only natural. Things do change in business, even dramatically. And that's going to happen in the future as well.

Gisbert Rühl

Gisbert is the former CEO of Klockner and Co., a steel manufacturer and one of the ten largest companies in Germany. He was a visionary in digitizing the distribution ecosystem for the steel industry way back in the early 2000s.

In this interview he talks about the challenges of digitizing a legacy company and handling the naysayers in his team. He feels that digitization needs two things—constant communication and regular training. He believes that any digital effort has to led by the CEO himself and not the chief digital officer or anyone in IT.

You saw the power of digital and pivoted Klockner to a digital system ahead of its time in the B2B business. What prompted you to do this? What were the signals?

Selling steel is a challenging business, with continuous pressure on margins. There are, on the one side, relatively powerful steel producers. On the other side, powerful customers.

And in the middle, a very fragmented distribution industry. And either this distribution industry must consolidate or something else should have to happen. Consolidation in our industry was not really taking place, because the advantages of being larger, for instance, on the procurement side, were too limited. Typically, fragmented industries start to consolidate at a certain point in time, but this was not happening. When we went public in 2006, we tried to consolidate the market through the acquisition of a couple of competitors. Others did this as well. But the margins didn't really improve. In 2013 I came up with the idea of a platform. My thinking, when I initiated the platform, was that it would be the most convenient way for the customer to buy steel through one interface through which the customer can buy all kinds of steel from all kinds of suppliers. This was the basic idea, and it was more or less the beginning of our activities.

The challenge was how to start. We really didn't know how to do it at that point in time, because there was no real blueprint for digitalizing a very traditional and conservative industry. We didn't want to make the same mistakes which happened in the steel space in 2000, when some producers started large projects to build some kind of platforms, invested a lot of money and failed. We wanted to do it differently. To find out how, I went to Silicon Valley and later on to Berlin, to learn how start-ups were doing it. Start-ups typically do not have that much money in the beginning and therefore have to do it in a very efficient way. And then we really learnt how to not only develop platforms but also how to make the business more convenient for customers. We learnt to really start with the customer and not with ourselves. Typically, corporations start when they want to optimize, when they want to build something, when they want to develop something with themselves. And we learnt that you have to start with the customer.

On the digital transformation front, what challenges did you face within the company, your own leadership team and from investors? What did you do to handle the naysayers?

Definitely, the problem existed. The stakeholders were not necessarily resistant, but they didn't believe in it. Neither the customers nor the suppliers believed in it. I would also say that our supervisory board, in the beginning, didn't believe in it. Very few believed in it. But by starting small, it was much easier for me to launch such an activity. We had a big goal, but we started small. And in a way, in the beginning, we were focusing on quick wins and showing that there was something which, when successful, could be scaled up. Our first platform was a contract platform. This was a relatively simple platform for the customer to organize the contract business with us better than in the past. After figuring out what was needed through customer ideation, we developed this relatively simple tool, and the customers liked it.

To motivate my people I told them, 'Look, in ten years from now, do you think our business will be the same as today, with all these new possibilities through technology?'

To inspire my people a lot of communication was necessary. We also initiated a digital academy for our people. But it was a process which took at least four to five years. While investors and analysts didn't believe in it at the beginning, I was at least able to convince them that this was something like a wild card—we don't invest too much money, and something could come out of that. In their research reports they were writing, 'We don't see any benefits right now. We also have no clue about how to calculate any benefits. But it could be something we don't know yet.' Today, convincing stakeholders to digitalize your business is, of course, much easier. People would probably say, 'Oh, why haven't you done it already?

The year 2013 was not early 2000 or late '90s. Digitalization had already proved its potential. So what were their key objections as far as this change was concerned?

In business, especially in traditional industries, digitalization was definitely not really taking place at that point of time. The CEO of a big German company told me once: 'You started with digitalization when we didn't know what this was.' There was still a lot of resistance. People were saying, 'In our industry, it will not work anyhow. We sell something different, like Amazon is selling. Customers want to talk with the sales guy and not buy online.' Furthermore, people in traditional businesses don't like change. It doesn't matter what kind of change you're driving; they don't want change.

Most of them want to have their nine-to-five job, and they want to keep the job as it is.

Convincing people to change is definitely not easy and takes time. Two things were extremely important to succeed finally. The right communication tool. In our case, it was Yammer from Microsoft. With Yammer I was able to get in touch with all employees, which is not possible with email or an intranet. I was also able to start a conversation with employees, whom I had never seen before. We were finally such an intensive user of Yammer that Microsoft was sending a team of twelve people to Klockner to film, for the Ignite conference, how we were using Yammer. Secondly, we initiated early on a digital academy where our people could do all kinds of courses to improve their digital know-how. We kept it voluntary; they could do it during working hours. As a result, the digital IQ of Klockner, as a whole, was continuously increasing. Today, Klockner is a company where many more employees, compared to any other steel company, know what digitalization means, how it works and what the benefits are. Finally, there was no one thing driving the change process. It took several measures to succeed in the end.

Did it at any point feel like your digital initiative was going south?

I never had any doubts. My thinking always was that when there is something more convenient for a customer than how we do it currently, change will happen somewhere down the road. Someone will provide a better solution for the customer, especially with all the technologies coming up and with all these exponential developments. It's going to come—that was my philosophy.

What personal lessons did you learn as you went through this digital transformation? What advice would you give B2B CEOs today on going digital?

My advice would be, do it, but do it differently from how it was done in the past. Think big and start small. Start with a small team, like a start-up. Start with an MVP (minimal viable product), try to find out the best solution, but always start with the customer. Don't think of your own benefits. Think only about the benefits for the customer. Pivot if necessary or even terminate a project if the chances of success are too low.

Any other personal takeaways that you had as you went through this digital transformation?

Every significant transformation has to be led by the CEO and not by a chief digital officer. In my thirty-five years in business, and about twenty-five years in management, I have participated in many change processes which have failed. Typically, transformations fail because the CEO is not seriously driving the process. Furthermore, communication is key. Every morning, for half an hour, I started looking at Yammer to find out what employees were most interested in and how I could contribute.

I think driving change is the most difficult part for management. It's much easier to manage a restructuring than a change process.

Anju Seth

Anju is an MBA from IIM Calcutta and did her PhD in strategy from the Ross School of Business, University of Michigan. She taught strategy at the University of Houston, University of Illinois Urbana-Champaign and Virginia Tech.

Anju was the first woman director at IIM Calcutta. In this interview she talks about the difference between educational institutions in India and America, the need for lifelong learning, the role of a board in an educational institution and how entrepreneurial professors will lead the change to a digital system in education.

You were involved with educational institutions in the US before you came to India to run IIM Calcutta. How different is it to manage an educational institution in the US from managing one in India?

In the US, there is a shared understanding on the part of various stakeholders—administrators and faculty, students and alumni, and government and society—of the mission of educational institutions and their key goals and objectives: to create a solid impact in research, learning, institutional building and outreach. Realistic benchmarking, with peer and aspirant institutions for continuous improvement in each of these areas, is essential. As is creating a fertile ground for team members to excel in their contributions to the mission. A fundamental requirement is good academic governance for transparency, accountability and meritocracy to earn the trust of all stakeholders and deliver the value they expect. Thus, in general, there exist mature governance systems with thoughtful policies that govern board members, key employees and the student body to clearly communicate a shared understanding, encourage commitment to the institution's mission as well as limit any potential conflicts of interest.

The top business schools in the US encourage the faculty to generate cutting-edge thought leadership in the creation of new knowledge; foster innovative teaching pedagogies that are the foundation of successful careers of students with life-long learning skills; and create executive education and entrepreneurial outreach programmes that can add true value to all participants.

So, in academic leadership positions in the US, my role was to provide vibrant leadership in sustainably propelling the institution to new heights for robust global and national impact. This included formulating and implementing strategy and policies jointly with my team while capitalizing on the unique strengths of the institution, generating and allocating resources, and relentless communication with stakeholders on the mission and progress of the institute. Strategic initiatives included continuous improvement of academic programmes and impact of faculty research, developing new growth opportunities with strong potential, hiring talented faculty in areas of strategic importance and capitalizing on valuable partnerships where necessary. Each initiative would be associated with desired metrics and realistic timelines for delivering results . . .

From my experience in India, it became evident that although many educational institutions have achieved maturity of vision to serve the needs of society with robust implementation, there also exists considerable variation. While some institutions voluntarily strive to better themselves in the spirit of enlightened self-interest, others appear to be content with the status quo, irrespective of any strategic imperatives, while ignoring or sidestepping fundamental norms of transparency and accountability.

As director of IIM Calcutta, how did you define your team for achieving institutional objectives? Was it faculty plus students plus the board, or just the faculty?

An educational institution is essentially an entrepreneurial entity, and its progress is defined by the innovative ability pursued with dedication and integrity of its team. I defined my team as not only faculty but also any members of staff, students and alumni, as well as senior officials of the Central and state governments. For any educational institution to create the desired impact requires encouragement and coordination among all the players with dedication to the desired goals. My role was to seed the idea and ensure fertile ground to encourage entrepreneurial volunteers with relevant expertise and the commitment to come together to take the idea forward.

IIM-C's response to the COVID crisis provides one example. In this unprecedented situation of lockdown, uncertainty and anxiety, numerous members of the faculty, administrators, officers, staff, board members, alumni and, notably, students, came together as a team to develop our response. During my tenure as director, the team not only successfully addressed the challenges of online classes but also ensured that most key academic processes, such as admissions, placement, salaries and payments to vendors, etc., were successfully accomplished without any serious spread of illness. None of this would have been possible without coordinated action to devise new solutions to unanticipated problems.

In the academic sphere, we created an innovative ecosystem to hone the skills of students in our degree programmes for careers in entrepreneurship while simultaneously assisting the entrepreneurial businesses supported by the IIM Calcutta incubator. A central feature of this initiative was the mentoring assistance of talented and dedicated alumni, faculty and student teams that worked jointly with the board and senior staff members of the incubator to facilitate learning-by-doing for students . . .

In all these initiatives, my approach was to seed the idea and scout around to build that team of individuals—whether faculty, staff, alumni, or students—who would be eager to contribute their talent and dedicated effort to taking the idea forward for successful implementation . . .

When you run an institution, how do you see the role of the board?

The most important aspect of a board member's role is their fiduciary responsibility to serve the institute's interest diligently and loyally. This responsibility is even more pointed in the face of institutional transformation.

First, being a fiduciary means that the board member is obliged to act *solely* in the interest of the institution. So, it is desirable that no board member is merely the representative of a particular interest group or allows any personal conflict of interest to colour their participation and actions. The structure of the board becomes crucial to consider; board members should be selected not only for their expertise but for their independence of thought and action.

Second, each board member should strive to be *well-informed* about both the challenges and opportunities inherent in transformation. What a board member doesn't know can hurt the institution!

Third, while the board's role is to oversee the CEO, it is also to *support* the management team and provide expertise and insight. Each board member brings potentially valuable knowledge to the table by virtue of their specialized background. But also, no member of the board should consider themselves the 'operating boss' with authority over the CEO.

Fourth, board processes should encourage *independence* of thought and informed debate and discussion. Obviously, reasonable people can disagree. So it is through the process of informed, open and engaged debate and discussion by individual board members that we build the openness that is integral to the complex task of institutional transformation.

The role of the board chairperson is particularly important. One concern in the model of split board chair–CEO structure, whether in a for-profit firm or a non-profit educational institution, is that it creates a lack of clarity as to who is in charge. The board chairperson's task is not to lead the organization (which is the task of the CEO) but rather, to *lead the board*.

Finally, the question arises: who monitors the monitor? As noted in the IIM Act, the board is supposedly accountable to the Ministry of Education, but more broadly, it is accountable to all the stakeholders of the institution. The requirement for integrity, transparency and accountability of the board is paramount. In addition, investing in rigorous board performance reviews can ensure that the board is not just enabled but required, through having the right people and right processes, to deliver on the desired institutional transformation.

Professors often talk of change, but they rarely change themselves and rarely do educational institutions change. Why do you think there is this contradiction?

In all the academic institutions that I have been associated with, entrepreneurial professors are often drivers of change, and we consider ourselves privileged to engage in such initiatives. Of course, it is also the case that many professors are most resistant to change. It is indeed ironic that these professors find it so difficult to practise what they preach! One simple explanation is the 'not invented here' syndrome: people adopt a negative attitude to ideas or technologies simply because they come from an external source. However, the explanation is likely to be more complex. All professors have encountered the situation where one academic group of 'insiders' takes charge of developing a change initiative, which is then subsequently shot down by another group of professors. Even if a meritorious proposal is adopted 'in theory', because the fact-based logical arguments in favour are so persuasive, it may never be implemented unless the responsibility, accountability and power to implement is specifically accorded and continuously monitored . . .

Whatever the structure of their pre-existing work 'norms', it is practically assured that proposals to significantly improve the quality of research or learning with transparency and accountability will appear to threaten important faculty endowments of some: their leisure time versus time allocated to institutional work, their recognition, security and status, the predictability of promotion and perquisites, and the safety of the status quo.

Because they are highly educated and articulate, they rationalize their fear and anxiety by providing arguments against or distractions from the proposals, often degenerating into ad hominem assertions and accusations of ulterior motives. Unsurprisingly, it is often those with the most invested in the threatened endowment who spearhead the charge in vociferously defending the status quo.

How do you think business education will get reshaped in a future digital world? What are the trends you see, and what capabilities do directors of business schools need to succeed in a digital world?

Technological developments are driving new opportunities for business education and value changes among customers. Digitalization is a key driver of change in that it enables the development of highly customized content and widens options for delivering learning material to students, including learning on demand.

Besides an intimate understanding of these requirements, directors of business schools need to have the capability and the autonomy to not only flexibly, speedily and effectively mount a response, but indeed to pre-empt opportunities that capitalize on the strengths of the institute and the specific needs of the marketplace. An important aspect of such initiatives is the capability to forge partnerships where necessary rather than attempt to do it alone, if one lacks key skills and capabilities that are essential for success.

For example, to respond to the emerging digital emphasis in higher education and to expand IIM Calcutta's international reach, my team entered a partnership with the online learning platform Coursera, to launch two certificate courses in our areas of strength, 'Management Science' and 'Supply Chain Analytics', for a global audience. The strategic intent was also to build on these certificates to create a new degree programme in business analytics for which Coursera had identified significant global demand. The proposal was value-creating for the institute in that it could add significant revenues to the institute, provide learning and development opportunities to faculty and doctoral students, and build strong networks with talented alumni as well as enable us to capitalize on and learn from Coursera's considerable capabilities.

Although the faculty body was given full autonomy to design the curricula, there was trepidation on the part of some professors. In the legacy environment, they had full control of what they taught, when they taught and even whether they taught a course, irrespective of the needs of the institute. Clearly, the new degree programmes would entail that our full-time professors develop new skills at first hand instead of teaching to a captive audience. Others were concerned about what would happen if there was no demand for their traditional course, if visiting faculty with greater teaching effectiveness could replace them, or how they would be compensated to teach in such programmes should they choose to participate in it.

Despite numerous efforts to allay fears and anxieties that prior 'endowments' would remain unaffected and that new proposals would create valuable opportunities for many if not all, the proposal attracted few enthusiasts from the faculty and little support from the board, despite numerous attempts on the part of my team to generate enthusiasm.

The world is changing and, for the sake of IIM Calcutta, it is my most earnest hope that the institute can keep up and excel. A model wherein success is measured only in terms of selection of talented students, their placements and the accomplishments of impressive alumni is unlikely to confer sustainable global leadership in the long run. In a world where there are more and more choices, the mere facade of excellence and lip service to global aspiration are just not enough. I am delighted to have created such opportunities for IIM Calcutta, and hope that it will be able to capitalize on them.

There is a general shift happening from degrees to skills. How do you see this impacting students and business schools in the future? How should a business school change for the future, in terms of revenues, teaching, fees and in terms of producing leaders for a different society?

The change in demand from degrees to skills that faces educational institutions has already yielded a healthy change in the nature of education itself. Perhaps the most fundamental change is a renewed emphasis on lifelong learning. The need of the hour is for businesses to assist learners to effectively perform in the context of work that has not yet been invented. The search for talent will be for individuals who are always seeking new opportunities in a spirit of inquiry, with strong problem-solving capabilities and the ability to translate skills into action. Thus, the truly successful business schools and students will accomplish the following five critical factors for their success:

1. Business schools will foster a spirit of inquiry to mentor students to develop both the capability and the desire for life-long learning. We need to encourage our learners to develop habits that deepen or expand their learning with resilience.

2. Closely linked is the notion of autonomy in learning, where the most successful students will take the initiative and responsibility for their learning.

3. The capability of students to translate skills into action is crucial. For students to hit the ground running, business schools will focus more on experiential learning outside the classroom, with more balance between learning-by-studying and learning-by-doing. Mechanisms include:

   • 'The flipped classroom', where simpler lecture material is online with more in-class focus on discussion of complex issues, interaction and application.

- Creating opportunities for partnerships with businesses, entrepreneurs and government agencies to solve real business or public policy problems.

4. Business schools, corporates and students can usefully work together to generate the capability for innovation and entrepreneurial approaches to new job creation. The new global reality means that managers and entrepreneurs have to develop a deep appreciation of wider societal and global issues to enable the co-creation of economic value and social value, and should seize opportunities that meet important needs and solve 'wicked' problems with speed and agility.

5. The unprecedented developments driven by the global pandemic will require perseverance and resilience (in addition to knowledge and skills) in effectively managing change. More than ever before, the world requires business leaders with strength of character and purpose, integrity and commitment to the greater good, as well as courage and confidence. Again, business schools, corporates and students can effectively work together in fostering such approaches to the broader learning experience.

Poonam Kaul

Poonam Kaul is one of the most passionate communications and marketing professionals. She started in advertising and then moved to Microsoft to run the communications function. She then moved to Nokia, where she made a significant impact with the brand through its glory days in shaping the narrative with her team as Nokia went from no. 77 to no. 1 on the Economic Times Most Trusted Brand list.

Poonam then worked at PepsiCo India and South Asia, managing communications and CSR. She pioneered the use of ORM (online reputation management). She then moved to Apple India to handle brand marketing and communications. She is actively involved with the start-up ecosystem and has helped NITI Aayog on a number of projects.

In this interview Poonam talks about the role of reputation and how social media is changing brand commentary.

How has company reputation become more important over the past twenty years?

Reputation management has played a significant role in most organizations, but over the last couple of years, it has become a lot more strategic as a function, especially with the advent of social media and smartphones that allow anyone to become a citizen journalist. Besides, there has been an unprecedented rise of social activism over the years. Organizations are always under the public scanner. All the more reason that the reputation of an organization is carefully nurtured as well as guarded constantly.

Therefore, investing in building reputation has never been as super critical as it is today. And it is not just about the organization any more—it's the people, partners, distributors, retailers, ecosystem, company values, etc. Everyone is contributing towards building a reputation every single day. Overall, while leadership paves the path for reputation, in today's world, it is important that everyone is singing from the same song sheet.

One wrong move, and you will end up fighting a losing battle. Warren Buffett had said years ago, 'It takes twenty years to build a reputation and five minutes to ruin it.' Extremely relevant today. And you see that every now and then, somebody's going down that path.

To manage and build a strong reputation, there are two words that might sound clichéd but are at the core of reputation management: consistency and persistence. Companies need to be at it consistently and persistently. Every single day. It's almost like you're chipping on something, you just have to continue chipping on it till it takes the shape you desire. And it takes a while to acquire that shape. Almost like sculpting. And building a reputation is never an overnight job, though people have started treating it like one. That's an incorrect approach.

Are employees ambassadors of the company they're a part of?

Reputation management is not just about PR or advertising or content marketing. It's also about how your people talk about you, how your people represent you outside. Every single public interface, every single salesperson, when they step out, they are your ambassador. Every person who's interacting with anyone outside the organization is your ambassador. How you leverage them then becomes important. Employees will talk respectfully and accurately about the company only when they are made aware of what is happening. That's why a robust internal communication system is necessary. It not only helps the employees speak accurately about the company, but also ensures that there is no scope left for those 'wink-wink, nudge-nudge' kinds of corridor conversations about the company, which usually arise from lack of clarity on some important issues related to the organization.

How important is it to have a balance between external and external communication?

These are two cohesive tracks. And both are important. However, in most organizations, internal communication is an afterthought, the lowest in the food chain. I believe it's one of the most strategic functions in communication. Communicating with your employees and other stakeholders is as important as talking to the external world, e.g., the media, analysts. Also, companies need to keep in mind that though these are not two parallel tracks, they need to be joined with each other. For example, if there is going to be a media release about a product launch, your teams need to know internally what is expected before they see it in the media . . . Internal comms are not only for disseminating good news, but also sharing not-so-good news. If there is a negative news cycle expected—for example, if the company is going for a headcount cut—it's important for people to know internally rather than seeing it on the front page of a newspaper. Sharing the perspective around bad news before it hits the press makes employees feel strongly about their organization and hence about their role in supporting it in dire times. That's the kind of balance companies require between internal and external comms.

Many CEOs believe that the media is unfair. What inputs would you have for CEOs about media and media interactions?

One big rule that needs to be broken is that just because you're running a business does not always mean that you're a great spokesperson. That also doesn't mean that you cannot become a great spokesperson. But one should remember that becoming a great spokesperson is a matter of discipline and practice. The one thing I have seen in all great spokespeople, global or nationally, is the amount of time they invest in sharpening their message and how they practise even after thousands of interviews like it's their first. That, for me, makes a great conversation with the media and more often than not results in great stories.

Additionally, I always advise CEOs/spokespeople to invest time first in building the narrative. That's what I did while preparing briefing documents for our spokespersons. I would push first at the base level and ask our internal teams, 'When this release comes out tomorrow, what headline would you want?' Think about it like that. Similarly, I would push the spokesperson and tell her/him that when you're having a conversation with a media person, think of the headline you're giving the media. If you just start talking about your 'great product' and throw in big data, the media guys will look at you and say, 'Just because it's a great product for you doesn't mean I am going to pick it up.' The conversation with them has to be more strategic and has to consciously deliver value. I have always believed that organizations should treat the media like a customer and explain things to them as you would to a customer, where you invest time in building the messaging and explaining the pros and cons. So why would you not do the same for media personnel? You are, at the end of the day, selling your product/service to them.

Secondly, you need to invest time in building relationships with the media. It's a symbiotic relationship. You give them information, and they will reach out to you when they need a viewpoint or perspective. And when CEOs say that the media doesn't treat them fairly, it's because they missed the point about investing time in them. They missed the point about investing time and talking to them about larger issues. You went to them only when you wanted a story and your PR team scheduled the interview. If you don't have a relationship with them, that reflects in the conversation as well as in the output the next day. We pioneered the concept of media offsites when I was at Nokia. We would invite the media for an interaction with the leadership team and while at one level, we would give them a perspective on the business, at another level, the objective was to build connections with them and break the ice. And it helped, always.

What is the impact of social media on company and brand reputation, and how did you manage ORM?

Social media has turned us into 'two-minutes noodles time'! Everything is instant. For consumers, it is about instant gratification. I see a picture, a comment or an article—I like or dislike. We don't wait for the postman any more; we wait for the blue tick on the message! From a brand perspective, at one level, social media gives you the platform to share news, updates—almost like a gateway into the organization. It also helps build a great engagement tool with consumers, stakeholders. But at another level, it is also a bit risky because everyone wants to be on social media—employees, partners, ecosystem. And that's fair because there is this psychological need for being 'visible' that social media caters/panders to. However, it is the responsibility of the comms team to build a framework that allows employees/stakeholders to leverage social media. It goes back to aligning employees, partners, stakeholders to the common vision, mission and the same song sheet. If that is in place, it is okay to let your employees and stakeholders do the talking. They can be your brand ambassadors. Some organizations do a phenomenal job of getting employees and partners to build authentic and organic content. That is a good zone to be in. However, social media also has its quirks; if there is no framework/guideline, then be prepared for hell to break loose any day.

Lastly, brands today face a lot of consumer/social activism on social media—they get trolled sometimes for big issues, but more often than not for irrelevant and obscure issues, where armchair intellectualism is at its best/worst. Therefore, as brand custodians, it is super important that when you put something out there, you are able to take the bouquets and the brickbats. In either case, it is important to stay true to your story. Being thick-skinned, if you are right, is important. Staying authentic plays a huge role in building positive sentiment and hence reputation on social media. Here, marketing and comms need to work jointly.

ORM, on the other hand, is a management tool. Almost like a lighthouse that keeps you posted around navigational challenges: which way the wind is flowing, rocky waters ahead, warnings and so on. Effectively, it helps you keep a pulse on what's going on—good or not so good. It helps you gauge sentiment, make changes, adapt and also understand where the next crisis may come from. It helps you differentiate between taking a proactive or reactive stance . . . But while ORM helps you address issues faster, you also need an efficient and proactive response mechanism built in to leverage it to the max. Plus, as brand custodians, keep a watchful eye on the narrative.

MNCs take a slow and methodical approach towards the media. Does this work in today's fast-content/news-cycle world?

A lot of responsibility to communicate with the media lies with the local team leadership. It's important for them to anticipate a situation, have a plan to deal with it, do scenario planning and get necessary approvals ahead of time from their global teams. Therefore, it is crucial to educate the global counterparts about your market and its challenges. Secondly, build trust with your global counterparts and don't give them surprises. That helps you not only with your current crisis but also any crisis that could come up in the future. That's what I did in my stints with MNCs like MSFT, PepsiCo and Nokia. All this happens when comms has a seat at the table.

In another MNC where I worked, there was no local spokesperson. Which meant that for everything, you needed to connect with the global entity. In such situations, you really miss out on putting out your local story.

Moreover, as I said, staying true to who you are, being authentic, being ahead of time, all these are very, very critical things for managing the media. There are times when you do well, and there are times when, despite all your planning and anticipation, you miss something, and the comms team needs to be prepared for that eventuality as well. It is an active 24/7 job, more so with social media.

Today, we have too many award ceremonies organized by too many people, some of them suspect. What advice would you have for companies on choosing which award platforms to participate in?

Anything that's paid for or is a paid opportunity should be avoided and discouraged. You lose credibility when you go for these paid awards. If it's an award that you paid for, it's not an award. We would also decline a speaking opportunity for our spokesperson if it was saddled with a sponsorship request. Our leaders need to be there because of who they are and what they represent, and not because we are paying for them to be there. And that goes back to building thought leadership for the organization and its leaders. Lastly, if you sponsor an event and be there to speak as a leader, that's a paid seat. Not authentic.

Managing Your Business: Points for Reflection

1. The past will not repeat itself. Stop extrapolating the past and start exploring ideas to renew your institution.
2. Technology will constantly reshape the world and will determine the heartbeat of an enterprise. Reskill the team to be tech savvy.
3. Institutional and individual reputation will matter and lead to better trust outcomes. Monitoring online reputation will be important.
4. A slow company cannot be agile, just as an agile company can never be slow. Agility is a combination of learning, forgetting, insights, alignment and processes. Agility will be the new competitive advantage.
5. A future world will not see longevity of companies or loyalty of employees. The average age of companies will be under twenty and average tenure in a company will be about 2–3 years. Think of both as you plan your career and life.

Acknowledgements

There are many people I want to thank for this book.

First, thanks to Sachin, who was so prompt and so good in doing the foreword.

Next, the twenty-one people who have contributed their time and thoughts. When I first reached out to them a year ago, all of them immediately accepted to be part of the book. When I sent them their specific questions, almost all of them got back saying, 'We need time. These are not easy questions, they are tough and need deep thought.' So each of them gave their best.

Thank You . . .

1. Aarti Kelshikar
2. Anju Seth
3. Anusha Suryanarayan
4. Babita Baruah
5. C.V.L. Srinivas
6. Devendra Chawla

7. Gautam Khanna
8. Gisbert Rühl
9. Harpreet A. De Singh
10. Harsha Bhogle
11. Hrishikesh Bhattacharyya
12. K.K. Sridhar
13. Nisha Narayanan
14. N.S. Rajan
15. Olli-Pekka Kallasvuo
16. Poonam Kaul
17. Renuka Ramnath
18. R.S. Subramanian
19. Shereen Bhan
20. Vikas Khanna
21. V.P. Malik

I want to thank the Penguin team—Radhika Marwah, my editor, for her patience, Vineet Gill, Vijesh Kumar, Anubha Jain, Prateek Agarwal, for all their help in the publishing of this book.

Thanks to Aarti Kelshikar, author of *How India Works*, who always played the role of the tough sounding board.

Thanks to Divya Karnal for compiling the data and the visuals.

Thanks to Vishwas Ved for doing all the interviews, editing them, running each interview past the interviewee and closing the interview. Vishwas, you were brilliant.

Thanks to Autumn Grey for the consumer research, for the cover design and all the work that will follow. Special shout-out to Karan Talreja, Kanchana Mohan, Mithun Cotha, Karthik Bhattarahalli and Ameena Khan.

Thank you, everyone. And thank you, dear reader—hope you found the book useful.